FINDING GENIUS IN THE AVERAGE ATHLETE

CHASING
THE GOAL

MICHAEL MURRAY

Chasing the Goal

Finding Genius in the Average Athlete

Michael Murray

For more information: mikepmurray25@gmail.com

ISBN Paperback: 978-1-962280-89-1

ISBN eBook: 978-1-962280-88-4

 Reflek
Publishing.

To my parents, who allowed me to chase my goal,
and to my wife and daughter,
who encouraged me to chase my new goal.

Table of Contents

Are You Average?

Average is what a failure claims to be when their family and friends ask them why they are not successful.

Average is the top of the bottom, the best of the worst, the bottom of the top, and the worst of the best. Which of these are you?

Being average means being run-of-the-mill, mediocre, insignificant, and an also-ran. A nonentity.

Being average is the lazy person's cop-out. It's lacking the guts to stand up in life. It's living by default.

Being average is taking up space for no purpose. It's taking the trip through life but never paying the fare. It's returning no interest in God's investment in you.

Being average is passing your life away with time rather than passing your time away with life. It's killing time rather than working it to death.

Being average is being forgotten once you pass from this life. The successful are remembered for their contributions, and the failures are remembered because they tried. But the average—the silent majority—are just forgotten.

Being average is committing the greatest crime you can against yourself, humanity, your God, and your *team*.

The saddest epitaph is this: "Here lies Mr. or Mrs. Average. Here lies the remains of what might have been, except for their belief that they were only average."[1]

Edmund Gaudet

---

1. John C. Maxwell, *The 15 Invaluable Laws of Growth* (Thomas Nelson, 2012), 196.

Preface

"Success is peace of mind which is a direct result
of self-satisfaction in knowing you did your best to
become the best you are capable of becoming."
—John Wooden, Legendary NCAA Basketball Coach

My daughter Georgia was my motivation for writing this book. When my wife Joy and I decided to start a family, we assumed it would be easy. My two older brothers, Bill and Kevin, and my sister, Deb, had no problems having kids. Same for Joy's sister. Among them, they had eleven children. We were pretty shocked that we were having problems. It never occurred to us that we would struggle.

The next five years of our lives seemed like Groundhog Day. Every month, we failed to conceive. It is hard to understand the frustration we felt and that there was no one to blame. We'd both been college athletes, and we were young and healthy, as far as we knew. It was just the luck of the draw.

We sought help from a fertility doctor. Three years in, we switched doctors, which gave us hope. After our fourth round of IVF failed, we had a pretty blunt conversation with the doctor. He told us that we had about a 5 percent chance of having a child. After taking a long pause to digest that news, Joy and I looked at each other and said that if someone told us we had a 5 percent chance of winning the lottery, we'd buy a ticket, right? With that, we decided to give it one last chance.

By the grace of God, six and a half weeks later, Joy was pregnant. But we weren't out of the woods yet. At our first ultrasound, there was no heartbeat. But the next week, there was. Then the baby wasn't measuring as expected but quickly caught up. At the eight-week mark, we were released to our ob-gyn. After five years of frustration and heartache, we were finally starting a family. We were absolutely ecstatic and couldn't wait to welcome a child into our universe.

I started writing this as a journal or diary through Joy's pregnancy because I didn't think we were ever going to have kids. It is hard to explain those feelings. Learning we were going to have a kid changed everything. We were eager to share with our child all that we learned growing up to make his or her life successful and maybe a little easier. It's probably every parent's dream to do so.

I never intended to turn my writings into a book. Instead, I thought it would be more of a story I could leave my children—just in case. Off and on over the next five to six years, I wrote some pages here and there. Without intending to, I stopped writing around the time my daughter started playing sports—most likely because I was teaching her my story in real time as I helped her through playing multiple sports.

One thing I never thought seriously about was coaching. I reluctantly fell into it after my daughter decided to follow her cousins Calleigh and Casey into hockey. It was never on my radar that Georgia would become a hockey player, and that was fine by me! She had told me on numerous occasions that she did not want to play hockey. I just took her to learn to skate a few days a month, more as a bonding experience between father and daughter.

I always knew I would share with Georgia stories about experiences that had impacted my life, but I never imagined teaching her what I had learned over the course of my sports career. Well, that changed the first time I put a stick in her hands when she was eight and had her play a pickup hockey game. She absolutely fell in love with it.

My life changed from that day forward.

Almost immediately, I was fully back into hockey and could not see my life without it. I had been out of the game for almost fifteen years. I had a love/hate relationship with the sport, which was complicated. On one hand, hockey had given me everything in life. On the other, it had also caused me the most pain. I went through a crazy journey, living out my dreams of playing professional hockey.

When it ended, I tried to push hockey away and move on to being a somewhat normal person. But something never felt right about it. The longer I was away, the more distance I felt from the sport. Always in the back of my mind, I felt that something was missing. I wished I could pass along the knowledge of how I became successful in sports. But, quite honestly, I didn't know how to do it.

When my daughter started playing, I quickly realized that I needed to get involved in the game and start coaching—something I had never really wanted to do. But the more I got involved, the more I realized how much the game had changed. Navigating the new hockey world was not easy, what with figuring out what team to be on, what coach to use, and whether we should play spring league or take a break. Hockey had become a for-profit business.

When I got into coaching, it was, in my opinion, for the right reasons. I wanted to share all the lessons I had learned to help make my daughter the best she could be. What happened next was unexpected. The lessons I was sharing with Georgia were now shaping the way I coached other kids. This was an unexpected by-product. Knowing that I have made an impact on some young athletes has been very rewarding.

I also realized that my experiences and philosophies could have an impact on some of my friends' kids, who were now in high school and trying to chase their own goals. A couple of friends of mine asked me to speak with their kids. It became clear to me that many high school kids struggle with the same things I did at that age.

There are plenty of coaches who are great at the X's and O's of the game. I believe that I am great at sharing what it takes to get the most out of your abilities, and that has little to do with the X's and O's. It is about trying to make the best version of yourself. That is the only goal, in my opinion.

As an adult, it is easy to see now what life is all about. I've always said that if you gave me the choice between living with regret or living with disappointment, I would choose disappointment 100 percent of the time. Disappointment simply means you did the very best you could and didn't accomplish what you set out to do. That is just part of life. Regret means you didn't try hard enough, that you didn't give it all you've got. Trust me, that's something you don't want to live with. You don't control the outcome of striving for a big goal, but you do control the process. That is how you live with peace of mind.

I've always felt that my story could help not only Georgia but any aspiring athlete. I was an average athlete who had a huge goal: to become a professional athlete at the highest level.

I never quite had the drive to finish writing the story I started when my daughter was born—probably out of fear of failure or the thought that no one would care. My motivation to turn this story into a book came in September 2023, when I was hit with a real health scare. I was rushed to the hospital by ambulance after coaching one of my daughter's hockey games. My world came crashing down on me without warning. I had absolutely no control of my balance system. After doctors evaluated me in the emergency room, they told me and my family that I was having a major stroke.

They left us with not much of a decision. They suggested that I take a very powerful blood thinner—tPA—which could either reverse the stroke and save my life or potentially kill me. It was not much of a decision in my mind or Joy's. Minutes later, they administered the medication and sent me to the intensive care unit (ICU) for observation.

Over the next twenty-four hours, I had great care. In my experience, when everyone at the hospital is extremely nice to you, you know you are in big trouble. I had been to this rodeo before. While I sat in the ICU for those twenty-four hours, waiting to have an MRI to confirm my stroke, I naturally contemplated life.

To say I was completely scared and depressed would be an understatement. I had no idea how I would function coming out of this. Walking seemed like the goal. Coaching did not seem to be in my immediate future. I made a lot of deals with the big guy upstairs. One of them was to look at my life and, once again, live with no regrets.

After a miserable twenty-four hours, the doctors took an MRI of my brain and found that I did not have a stroke after all. The initial relief was followed by the uncertainty of the diagnosis. I still could not walk and felt horrible. After two days, the doctors released me from the hospital to figure it out on my own.

It took several months to rule out a lot of bad stuff—like MS, a tumor, or an undiagnosed stroke. Finally, the doctors figured out that I had a rare form of vertigo—vestibular neuritis. Unknown to me, the shingles virus had attacked and damaged my vestibular nerve, which connects the inner ear to my brain. It also controls balance.

As I was struggling to get back to health, I couldn't help but think about the deals I'd made while sitting in the ICU. I had a lot of time on my hands to contemplate life. There are times when things become crystal clear. This was one of those times.

So, I decided I would turn my story into a book and hopefully have a greater impact by extending the audience. Finishing this decade-and-a-half-long project would be one less thing to check off on my bucket list. Otherwise, I would likely live with regret.

Here we go.

Introduction

"It was the best of times, it was the worst of times . . ."
—Charles Dickens, A Tale of Two Cities

December 28, 1995. There I was, sitting in the visiting locker room, sweat in my eyes, tears streaming down my face, and blood coming from my nose. I was trying to wrap my brain around what had just happened. In a span of ten minutes, I'd fought two of my teammates, one of whom was my best friend on the team. The fight had consisted of bare knuckles and bone smashing bones. Absolute fury.

That's life trying to make it in professional sports.

We'd had a particularly heated practice the day after a lackluster loss to our rivals, the Fredericton Canadiens. Before practice, the coach did his best Herb Brooks impression and singled me out in front of the team. I was a captain, and the coach wanted to make a point. If he could call me out, then he could do it to anyone.

The only problem was that he didn't let me in on the secret. Well, I was furious. I was one of the only ones playing physical the night before, and I was upset at being singled out. I set foot on the ice for practice with an extra hop in my legs.

The coach decided to run a series of contact drills, and things started to get out of hand. On one drill, I flew in and slammed a French-Canadian teammate into the boards. He didn't like it and decided to chase me up the ice. I turned around at center ice and noticed he was yelling at me. I dropped my gloves and let him have it, pummeling him with my bare knuckles as others tried to break it up.

To our amazement, the coach insisted that the drill continue around us. After a few minutes, we stopped, and I went back in line. My teammate had to go to the trainer and get stitched up.

My next time up in the drill, I raced down and slammed my roommate cleanly into the boards. I was still fired up from the fight. He didn't like it so much either. The next time up, I was racing in and about to hit my roommate again when he stopped short and elbowed me in the face. Without hesitation, I dropped my gloves and went bare knuckles again. We exchanged blow for blow.

Guys jumped in to break it up, but the damage was done. Both of us had bloody noses, swollen faces, and cut-up knuckles. Not only did I fight my roommate to a draw, but he would later go on to be one of the toughest guys in the National Hockey League (NHL). I took off my helmet and smashed it to pieces. I left the ice and had to go back to the locker room to get another helmet.

At that point, I had lost my mind. As I stepped back on the ice, the team had been split up into two zones and was working on different things. I just skated around the neutral zone with my stick clenched in my hands. We probably stayed on the ice for another five minutes. I just paced around the neutral zone, waiting for anyone to approach me. I was seeing absolute red in my eyes.

If anyone got close to me, I was prepared to butcher them with my stick. It was funny because I think everyone knew that, including the coaches. Everyone just stayed clear of me and left me alone. Thank God, because I was prepared to do it.

I certainly left my mark on that practice. Soon after, the coach decided that was enough and kicked us off the ice.

I was still so upset about what happened that I went into the visiting room to ice my face and calm down. A few minutes later, the coach came into the locker room and wanted to talk with me. Even though I was one of the assistant captains, this was not an everyday occurrence. He ruled by fear and seemed to love being that way. In this instance, the rare human side of him came out.

The coach decided to have a heart-to-heart with me. He told me how he once fought his best friend at practice (the Calgary Flames general manager) and traveled home together afterward. He said their friendship became stronger. He told me my reaction on the ice that day was exactly why my teammates liked and respected me so much. A few weeks earlier, the coach had polled the players, and I was voted the best player on the team. I guess that backfired because moments later, he announced that Calgary had recalled one of my teammates, to play his first NHL game.

My teammate was a former first-round bust who was having a decent year. And the powers-that-be decided to call him up. Regardless, this was my first inclination that my dream of playing in the NHL was truly within reach. The coach said I was leading the team in minutes played and was our most dependable player.

The next thing that came out of his mouth left me speechless, making this day even more surreal than it had already been. The coach told me I was the next player being called up to Calgary, to the NHL. There was nothing official yet, but it could happen any day. Now leading up to this, I'd heard from several teammates who recently returned to Saint John from Calgary—as well as my agent, who heard it through the grapevine, had told me this as well. To hear it directly from the coach's mouth solidified the message. My outlook changed completely in that instant.

As he left the room, I sat there stunned. It is almost impossible to describe that feeling—knowing how close I was to finally reaching my dream. The range of emotions, going from homicidal to absolute elation in a matter of minutes, is mind-blowing. How can you put into words hearing that your wildest dreams that you've had since you were a kid were coming true? Some people grew up wanting to be the president of the United States, an astronaut, a famous actor, or musician. From as early as I can remember, I wanted to play in the NHL. Now it was about to become my reality. I sat in that locker room reflecting on the long road I'd traveled to get here. The struggles, painful injuries, and the internal and external doubts.

My successes didn't come without tremendous challenges. I had to find the pathway largely by myself. By reading this book, I am hoping you don't have to go through as many struggles as I went through as a teenager. I hope you don't have to learn the hard way. You may see some similarities between my stories and what you are going through now.

I hope this story will help you with some of the inevitable challenges you will face in life. I have a unique perspective as an adult as I look back now on what made me successful and helped turn an average athlete into a professional.

As I was about to begin my senior year of high school, I realized time was running out. Up to that point, I had not been ready for that phase in my life. I had not accomplished anything of significance and realized that I had reached a critical point. Up until then, I'd been a big dreamer. I had ideas about what I wanted to become but had no plan for how to get there. At that age, it is hard to comprehend the value of time, but I suddenly had a tremendous sense of urgency and an awareness that this was time I could not get back.

Time is a funny thing. When you are young, summers seem to last forever, and a high school career seems to last for a decade. Only from the perspective of middle age do you realize how quickly time goes by and that you need to take advantage of opportunities when you can. Four years at my age seems like a long weekend.

My gift in high school was not necessarily my athletic ability but a slight comprehension of time. I understood that I did not want to look back ten years later and regret that I hadn't done everything possible to achieve my dreams.

I only had one life to live.

Each day, you are writing your own story, whether you like it or not. When you look back ten, fifteen, or twenty years from now, are you going to be proud of what you wrote down in your book? If you can understand that concept, you are already ahead of your competition.

When I look back on why I had a successful career and others didn't, there is a pretty simple explanation. I simply outlasted people. I sought out and listened to advice on how to get better. I was curious about how others were successful. I read biographies, *ESPN The Magazine*, and *Sports Illustrated*, and I watched every sports movie I could.

I was very competitive but also stubborn. I refused to quit when everything in the universe was telling me to. The way I looked at it, there is a clock on your athletic career. Eventually, time will run out.

Focus on what you can do today. Logically, the only thing you can control is now! If you focus on that, the results will be the results. You will have peace of mind because you did everything you could to be the best you could be. You will learn as you get older that it will be enough.

Trust me.

There was one pivotal moment heading into my senior year of high school that catapulted me into having a life-changing year. I was able to draw on experiences that had shaped me throughout my childhood and used this new message to set myself on a path that I dreamed of. All these experiences that I put into my memory bank were like compound interest that I pulled from throughout my sports career.

Here is how it all started.

Chapter 1
Growing Up

"Do you believe in miracles? YES!"

—Al Michaels, Miracle on Ice

I grew up on the heels of the Bobby Orr era in New England. New rinks were being built all around the area, and it seemed that every town around us had a strong hockey program. All communities were hockey-crazy, and everyone I grew up with wanted to play for the Boston Bruins.

One of my earliest memories that helped set the direction of my life was the 1980 USA Olympic ice hockey team. The Miracle on Ice captivated everyone I played with and, ultimately, even those who weren't hockey fans. The USA team was a group of college kids facing off against the greatest team in maybe the history of hockey. A few months earlier, the Soviet Union team had dominated a team of NHL all-stars 6–0. Team USA beating the Soviets was considered the greatest upset in modern sports history. My dream was not necessarily to just play in the NHL but also to play for the US Olympic team. I was obsessed with and inspired by that unbelievable achievement.

"Do you believe in miracles?"

I did.

Even with the lure of hockey in those days, I had a split sports personality. I wanted to be the heavyweight champion of the world, catcher for the Boston Red Sox, quarterback of the University of Notre Dame, and a hockey player.

No doubt, my love of sports came from my father. He was a great athlete in his own right. He'd grown up in Bayside, Queens, New York, and I loved hearing his stories about playing against Major League Baseball Hall of Famer Carl Yastrzemski and the Torre brothers when he was growing up. He also played multiple sports—football, baseball, soccer, and basketball. Interestingly, he didn't play hockey until he moved up to Rhode Island before I was born.

I was an obsessed sports fan because of that upbringing.

I don't view myself as anything more than your average kid. When I look back on my life, I see a few moments in which I know played a pivotal role in any success I had. I built a memory bank of pivotal moments in life that went on to help me as times got tough.

I had an idyllic upbringing and was raised by loving parents as the fourth of five children. Money was always tight, but that never seemed to prevent us from doing anything. Hand-me-downs were the financial strategy my parents perfected. My father had a ridiculous work ethic, regularly leaving by five thirty a.m. and returning home by seven p.m. It seemed like every family that lived in my neighborhood of Rolling Acres had the same family structure.

We were able to roam our neighborhood and find a competitive sport being played at any moment. There were lots of great athletes and plenty of competition. It was our version of what is now for-profit club sports.

I played every sport imaginable and had a brother, Kevin, who was three years older than me, whom I emulated. I also had my younger sister, Beth, who followed me around and was always willing to throw on the goalie equipment so I had someone to shoot on. Having a brother who was three years older than me and played the same sports gave me an advantage. We fought endlessly, and I never backed down. I was able to hone my athletic ability, toughness, and competitiveness because of him. I absolutely hated losing, and everyone knew it. Especially him. He has the bite marks to prove it.

We had many athletes from the neighborhood who went on to play high school and college sports. Five of us played for our high school hockey team. Playing in street hockey tournaments, setting up pond hockey in the winters on Mooney's pond, and shooting pucks in my driveway led to the development of very good hockey players in Rolling Acres.

But my sports career was almost over before it started.

I was ten years old, was playing defensive back in Pop Warner football, and had no fear. That quickly changed one Sunday when we played a team from Pawtucket. Early in the game, their huge running back came through the line, and I dove headfirst at his knees. Obviously, I hadn't learned the proper tackling technique and subsequently snapped back my head and neck. I still vividly remember the sheer panic. I couldn't breathe or move. It was like a dream as everyone stood over me talking to me, but I couldn't hear a thing. I was fighting to breathe and move any part of my body.

My parents happened to be a few minutes late and walked in as the rescue team was loading me into the ambulance. I'm sure they were as panicked as I was and followed me to the hospital. Everyone at the hospital was being overly nice to me. I learned later in life that this was not a good thing.

The doctor would come in every fifteen minutes or so and scratch the bottom of my foot with a key to see if my feeling had come back. My parents tried to hide the desperation on their faces. They had summoned their closest friends, the Lynches, to the hospital because they were sure that I was paralyzed. It seemed like I couldn't feel anything in my legs for hours. Eventually, the doctor came in and scratched my foot one last time, and it finally jumped.

A huge sigh of relief came over me and the room.

The doctor described it as spinal shock and said I would be out of contact sports for at least six months. Since I was so competitive, it was complete torture for me. I did come back a little early and participated in a hockey clinic. I collided with another player midway through the practice and experienced a minor relapse of the pain.

And I was out another three months.

In some small way at that age, I learned that sports could be taken away at any moment. The following football season, I returned to the team a completely different player. I was petrified to hit someone with the force I once had. I lasted the rest of the season but did not enjoy the experience. I didn't play football again until I entered high school. This time, I was a quarterback.

The early 1980s in northern Rhode Island was an exciting time to play hockey. The Mount Saint Charles (MSC) hockey team dominated the 1980s by winning ten straight national high school hockey championships. Anyone in my area who was any sort of hockey player went to MSC, also called the Mount. Their hockey games were Rhode Island's version of *Friday Night Lights*. It was nearly impossible to get tickets.

The players were treated like rock stars, and for good reason. In 1983, MSC had future number-one NHL draft pick Brian Lawton. They also had 1984 Olympian Paul Guay. It seemed that almost every player in those days either was drafted or went on to play Division 1 college hockey. In Rhode Island, high school hockey stars played for one of the big three schools, with Bishop Hendricken High School and La Salle Academy being the others. Hockey players where I grew up who wanted to have a career in the sport went to MSC.

My high school team practiced in the same rink as MSC. The aura or attitude that came from that program was obvious. When we walked into the rink before our practice, we were not allowed to look at the ice as they were practicing. If we did, the coach went ballistic and screamed at us.

It was such a secretive place and, quite honestly, had so much misplaced arrogance that you couldn't help but feel like a second-class hockey player if you didn't play for them. They definitely looked down on us as public school players. Quite frankly, it pissed me off. Their attitude definitely had an impact on me. It fueled my desire to play at the highest levels and prove everyone wrong.

Going to MSC was the obvious and practically only path to hockey stardom, and the players they produced proved that over and over. But there were a few problems for me. First, I have what you may call a split sports personality. As much as I loved playing hockey and wanted a career in it, I also played multiple sports in their respective seasons. I wanted to play football, and MSC did not have a team.

My dad was big on playing sports in their season, and this did not allow me to fully concentrate on just one. This also presented a challenge because football directly competed with hockey in the fall. For much of my high school career, I didn't step on the ice until the day after Thanksgiving due to my football schedule. It put me at a great disadvantage compared to the players who were on the ice starting in September. They were getting at least twice as much ice time in those crucial development years.

Second, the principal of Cumberland High School (CHS) was Mr. Lynch. And he was my dad's best friend—someone I considered a mentor. My parents wouldn't even consider sending me to MSC, and I did not push them on it. I wanted more than anything to impress Mr. Lynch by attending CHS.

Sure, he was a great academic, but he was also an athlete, coach, and mentor. He played quarterback at Boston College and became a college coach at Providence College. He was a long-time high school principal and superintendent and eventually ran the Rhode Island Interscholastic League. He raised three daughters and a son who were all great athletes. His son went on to play quarterback at the University of Rhode Island, and I idolized him.

It was even more important to me that Mr. Lynch see me not only as a hockey player but a great athlete. He went on to have a great influence on me and induct me into the Cumberland High School Athletic Hall of Fame—one of my biggest honors as an athlete.

During middle school, I was considered one of the best players in my age group in Rhode Island. I was selected to Team Rhode Island on two occasions, and we competed in the Yankee Conference Championship, which brought together New England's best players in our age group.

When it was time to choose a high school, most of my hockey friends went to one of the big three. I, however, chose a different path. My hockey friends couldn't believe that I would pass up a chance to play at the Mount. By making this choice, I knew my road to a career in hockey would be a long shot at best. But I held on to the belief that if I was as good as the others were in middle school, I could, with perseverance, eventually be as good as them, if not better, when it mattered— in college and beyond.

I played football, hockey, and baseball all four years of high school. I was the starting quarterback on the freshman football team, started for the varsity hockey team, and played catcher for the baseball team. Everything was going as planned, as I was excelling at all three sports. But early in my sophomore football season, everything changed.

I was the backup quarterback for a senior, and the varsity team was struggling. During the homecoming game against Hendricken, we were losing. The coach decided to start me for the second half. I helped rally the team and drove us down for a few scores. We ended up losing, but I made enough of an impression that the coaches planned to start me the next week for my first varsity start.

I was fired up for the opportunity.

There was only one problem. I had to play in the junior varsity game the Monday after the game at Hendricken. A few plays into that game, which was on a rainy morning, I handed off to one of our running backs. He took a few steps and fumbled the ball. I turned around, saw the ball on the ground, and instinctively bent over to pick it up. My plan was to run with it. But as I was bent over it, the opposing defensive end jumped on my back and drove my knee into the ground. The pressure snapped my femur in half.

I can still feel it to this day. I knew something was wrong, and I couldn't move off the ground. My head was face down in the mud, and I kept waving over to the bench to come get me. The coach kept looking at me and motioning to get up. But it wasn't happening. I heard later that fans in the stands said they could hear the crack of the bone from their seats. The medical staff came out and tried to move me. Instantly, I was in excruciating pain. The only thing I can compare it to is having a baseball bat smashed in your face.

My parents showed up just as the ambulance was pulling onto the field. It was the second game in my life that they were late to, and it was déjà vu. (We later agreed that if they were late to a game again, they would turn around and leave. My dad just decided to show up hours early for each game instead.) I was lying on the field, and everyone was being really nice to me. They were trying to convince me that maybe I'd just dislocated my knee. I would believe anything at that point.

The ambulance took me to the hospital anyway.

Unfortunately, it was Columbus Day, and the backup crew was on at the hospital. They put me in traction, but I was still in excruciating pain for hours. When they took an X-ray, I happened to look over at an image of a bone snapped in half. I didn't even realize it was my leg. I was still convinced I had a dislocation.

As I was lying in the waiting room in pain, a doctor walked in, took one look at my traction, and realized it was on wrong. He quickly grabbed a few doctors, then grabbed the bottom of my leg and pulled it out. Instant pain led to instant relief. The pain had been coming from nerves touching each other. The staff put weights on my foot to hold it there and got me prepared for surgery. They inserted a rod into my leg from my hip to my knee, which would stay there for the next one and a half years. I stayed in the hospital for a week before returning home and starting my long rehab.

As a result of my broken femur, I missed the rest of the football season and the majority of the hockey season. But I was back on the ice about three months after the injury and was ready to play the last few games and the playoffs. I was certainly less than 100 percent, but I was able to score a goal in the state championship final game.

After the season, I went on to play in and win the Bantam New England Ice Hockey Championship for my club team, the Woonsocket North Stars. I was still not close to being 100 percent from my broken femur but was able to play at a pretty high level.

The one thing from that tournament that stuck with and influenced me for years to come was a crushing failure. We were in the national semifinals, playing against a team from South Bend, Indiana. It was a back-and-forth game that ended up going into overtime. A few minutes into overtime, our defenseman flipped the puck out of our zone and into theirs. I raced after the puck but was trailing the defensemen by a few steps. As the defenseman caught the puck, I was right on him. Around the top of the circle, I lifted his stick and stole the puck. I was right on top of the goalie at that point and deked around him. The net was open, and I quickly shot the puck before I ran out of room. The puck rang off the crossbar and into the opposite corner. Shortly thereafter, they came down, scored the overtime winner, and knocked us out of the national championship game.

I was crushed. I'd had a chance to send us to the national championship game, and that feeling of failure stuck with me for a long time. What I did with that failure would ultimately shape who I would become as an athlete.

I turned it into fuel.

I used that fuel to work even harder at being the best I could be. I worked out harder, shot more pucks, and was determined to never be on that side of the game again. It would pay huge dividends for me only a few short years later and was just another addition to the memory bank.

Going into my junior year, I decided, without much thought, to play football again. I wanted to be the starting quarterback and earned the opportunity to do so. The hockey team and coaches didn't think it was a great idea, but I didn't really care what they thought. I loved playing the game, and the majority of my friends were on the team.

The season got off to a slow start because I came down with mononucleosis, which knocked me out of the first few weeks of the season. But I gained back the starting job midway through the second game of the season. We were playing the powerhouse Rogers High School. I rallied the team in the second half but ultimately fell short in the last play of the game. We lost two of our first three games of the year by close scores but went on to win the last seven games in convincing fashion—including beating the eventual state champion and our Thanksgiving rival, Woonsocket High School.

One game that year helped change the way I felt about sports. We were getting ready to play the undefeated and eventual state champion, Cranston East High School. On my way home from practice one day that week, I was dropping off a friend and drove by my neighbor, Mr. Krebs, running on Mendon Road. He had recently gotten into running to get into better shape. I beeped at him and waved. I noticed how miserable he looked running but didn't think much about it.

As I pulled down my street about thirty minutes later, I noticed my sister and a neighbor standing in the middle of the street. I jokingly drove at them, but they didn't budge. I could tell something was wrong. When I jumped out of my car and ran over to them, my sister started crying. Mrs. Krebs had screamed out to Beth moments earlier to call 911.

Mr. Krebs had dropped dead of a massive heart attack.

It was surreal to remember that I'd just seen him running thirty minutes earlier. I learned that he'd arrived home from his run, walked into the kitchen, and collapsed to the floor. Ambulances, police cars, and fire engines quickly arrived at the scene, but it was too late. Ironically, my dad came home early that day—which never happened—because he was taking us to the US Olympic team vs Providence College game that night. He had raced into the Krebs house to help, to no avail.

Mr. Krebs was a close friend of our family and the first person close to me who died. He had planned to come to the game and see me play football that Saturday, and it was going to be his first time. He was a very unique person to me. An avid outdoorsman; a hunter and fisherman who had fun with the best of them. Always the life of the party. While he had his evening cocktails on his porch, he would yell at me as I shot pucks, played basketball, or engaged in any of the numerous sports I played. I guess he got a kick out of watching me.

His death had a profound effect on me, and I still think about it often. I was stunned that he passed away. Attending my first wake, kneeling in front of his casket, and seeing his signature cowboy hat was chilling. That was when his death really hit me. I started to cry when we returned to the car and couldn't stop for hours. As I sat in my bedroom that night, I decided to dedicate the game against Cranston East to Mr. Krebs.

When I woke the next morning, I had this very odd, focused feeling. It was decided, by my parents, that my family would go on to the funeral without me. I pulled my dad aside to tell him that I was dedicating the game to Mr. Krebs. I was very upset that I couldn't attend the funeral, but he assured me it was okay and that everyone would understand.

I don't remember telling anyone on the team what had happened. But what transpired on the field that day changed my life and career. It was the first time I felt someone else take over my body. It was either God or Mr. Krebs. Or maybe both. I had an out-of-body experience and felt as though I was watching myself play from above.

I had unlimited energy and complete hyper-focus during that game. I was in a zone. But, to be honest, it was more than that. I may not be the most religious person in the world, but I am more spiritual now because of it. I went on to chase that feeling for the rest of my career. Having that moment-to-moment focus like I had that day would end up being a staple in my career and helped me perform at my best in critical situations.

We were heavy underdogs against the Cranston East Bolts. We went on to completely dominate the eventual state champion by a score of 36–16. I had a day I will never forget. I was 12–16 passing, more than two-hundred-and-fifty yards, and three touchdown passes. And I ran for a sixty-five-yard touchdown. The touchdown run was the most surprising of all. I was coming off a broken femur a year earlier and was one of the slowest players on the team. I ran through and by Cranston East's whole team for a sixty-five-yard score.

It is hard to explain the feeling that overcame me. I still get chills thinking about it. Later, I was named the Rhode Island athlete of the week for all sports.

After the game, I went to the Krebs house for the collation. When I walked in the door, Mrs. Krebs came right over to me. In her time of sorrow, she thanked me for dedicating the game to him and said he would have been very proud of me. I carry his obituary with me to this day. It traveled with me to college and the pros. I look at it and remember how fragile life is and how much power we have inside us.

My high school went on to finish the season with what I believe was the best team in the state. Unfortunately, only one team from each division made the state championship game. There was no playoff system back then. We capped off the season with a 36–6 pounding of our Thanksgiving rival, Woonsocket.

The next day, I was on to hockey season.

But I didn't have much time to prepare. The first time I went on the ice was the day after Thanksgiving. That was pretty much unheard of for someone who wanted to be a good hockey player, never mind an elite one. Still, in my junior year, we won our second consecutive Met B-3 championship. I was the leading scorer of the team and second in the state.

Baseball season followed, and I started at third base for an average team. I had a very successful junior season on the playing fields, but it was nothing outstanding. I was underperforming in the classroom and got a wake-up call that changed my focus leading into the summer.

Shortly before the school year was out, I was called down to the principal's office. When I walked into Mr. Lynch's office, he was not smiling at all. Frankly, he was disappointed in me. He knew I did poorly on the SAT and that my grades were not much different. He told me that I wasn't leaving myself many options for college. It didn't matter how well I did in sports if I didn't turn it around in the classroom quickly.

There wasn't a worse feeling than disappointing someone I was eager to impress. But it was probably the best thing that could have happened to me at that moment. It was the slap in the face I needed to focus on the biggest year of my life.

Going into the summer before my senior year, the football coach, Tim Coen, decided to change our offense from the wing-T to the wishbone. The wishbone is a run-first offense. As I mentioned earlier, I was a slow runner and thought Coach was crazy. But, then again, he might have been a genius. We had lost our entire offensive line, and it was being replaced with players who were smaller than me. The key to the offense was having linemen who only had to chop blocks. They weren't required to hold blocks long because misdirection was the objective.

I trained all summer with one of our assistant coaches, who was also a boxing trainer. He trained me to box at the local Boys and Girls Club, which included jumping rope, heavy bag, and speed bag work. They were the toughest workouts of my life.

He often got me up at four in the morning to go running at Lincoln Woods. The first morning, he asked me, "Do you know why we are working out this early in the morning?" When I said no, he replied, "Because nobody else is doing it." That still sticks with me. The quote he wrote on one of my workout programs was "You can't measure a guy's heart." I still have it in my office.

I was on a mission all summer to be in the best shape of my life and have an unforgettable senior year. But I'm not going to lie and say I wasn't concerned about my health and safety heading into the football season. I knew that my destiny was to play college and pro hockey, and it was hard not to think about how I'd broken my femur in my sophomore year. The fact that we had a small offensive line and I was going to run a run-first offense put me in harm's way.

However, it did motivate me to train all that much harder. I didn't want to disappoint my teammates. Besides, I loved playing football. Most of my friends were on the team. Years later, many of them would be in my wedding party and continue to be my lifelong friends.

Chapter 2
Senior Year

"God must have loved the average man because
he made so many of them."
—Bob Richards

I t was the night before the first day of school in my senior
year. I was sitting in bed, thinking about what my future
had in store for me. I'd put in a tremendous amount of hard
work in the weight room and on the ice over the summer,
and I was ready. There was no doubt I realized that the real
world was coming quickly, and I was a little frantic to leave
my mark by the end of my high school career. Let's be clear:
I was probably like most seventeen-year-olds who are filled
with anxiety and trying to figure out life.

Having always been a dreamer, I set big goals for myself.
But reflecting on my high school career, I could see that I had
accomplished very little. I was a good athlete but had not
dedicated myself in the classroom. I had put myself behind
the eight ball. Another year like this would not get me to the

promised land of college and pro hockey. What was I going to do? How was I going to separate myself from the pack of other hockey players my age?

I was aware that I didn't want to live with regrets and that time was running out. The regret of not trying to accomplish all the dreams I'd had since childhood seemed like a horrible thing to live with. I was determined to do everything in my power to give hockey my absolute best shot. So I made a deal with myself that this was the year I would make my mark and leave my legacy.

Then fate or divine intervention stepped in and gave me the last piece to the puzzle that connected all the dots for me. This helped turn the skills that I'd developed over the summer into the belief that I needed to accomplish great things.

As I sat there, staring at all my goals posted on my walls, I noticed a tape cassette in my stereo that I hadn't noticed before. Curiosity got the better of me, so I walked over and decided to play it. The voice that came over the speaker entranced me. I have no idea how the tape got there, even to this day. I assumed it was my brother's, but for some reason, I never asked. It transformed my thought process from that day going forward.

There is genius in the average man. That was the theme of the motivational tape I'd stumbled onto. I listened for around an hour, but it seemed to be just a minute. Former Olympian Bob Richards was the man behind the voice. And I had my aha moment. Everything seemed to make sense. This was the playbook and road map I was going to live by. He talked about how God must have loved the average man because he made so many of them and how the average star athlete is just five ten and 185 pounds.

Well, I was bigger than that.

Bob said he believed that there is genius in everyone. Even though nature endows us with inborn abilities and traits, it doesn't mean they are always available to us. You have to find them in yourself. According to him, 99 percent of people used 1 percent of their capacity. If you could use even 5 percent of your capacity, imagine what you could accomplish. You can do this only by being motivated.

Bob regarded motivation as the most important work in the history of man. He explained that motivation is behind everything that happens. A wheel doesn't turn unless a person is motivated. A person doesn't make it to the top unless they are motivated. Edison said, "Genius is 1 percent inspiration and 99 percent perspiration." To be great in the sports world, you have to put in effort and work.

It is a language of self-reliance, which means relying on your own efforts and abilities rather than depending on others for help. I knew that to be successful in my senior year and accomplish all my dreams, I would have to be self-reliant. Nobody was going to run the race for me.

When you step into the batter's box, you're all alone. You either strike out or hit, depending on your ability and not someone else's. You can't fake the question. You can't give yourself putts. When you're out there running, the stopwatch tells you exactly how fast you're going. You go over that crossbar, or you don't. It stays up, or it comes down. You have to look yourself in the eye. You are not great in sports unless you yourself do it.

"If you want to be a champion, you need to analyze yourself. You need to recognize your weakness and change your weakness into power." There isn't a person who has lived who hasn't had a weakness of one kind or another. The sports world does not tolerate weakness. You don't blame someone else for your shortcomings. You turn your weakness into power.

Bob went on to say that you won't meet a more mediocre guy than him. He was five ten and weighed 185 pounds. He had an average brain and an average voice. If he could be a champion and a famous speaker, he said, what could you do with your super-average abilities?

I bought every line. I was fully in.

There is no question that making the decision and commitment to live without regrets set me on a path to success. I'd already had the road map, and now I had the fuel to make it happen. The key was to find the belief and motivation to push me when it got hard. And believe me, it got hard. Listening to the tape every night filled my tank to conquer the next day. It was fate that the tape dropped in my lap. Once you find your road map, you need to find your own "tape" to make it happen.

I set very clear goals for myself and posted them on the walls so I could see them every night. I also set goals around who I didn't want to be. I still remember most of them:

1) Win a state championship in football.
2) Be the first team all-state quarterback.
3) Win a state championship in hockey.

4) Average three goals a game.

5) Be all-state in hockey.

6) Don't be another "Joe Smith."

(Joe Smith is a compilation of people I knew who might have been more talented than me but made poor decisions and gave me an opportunity to succeed. I am sure every town has a Joe Smith.)

The morning after I found the tape, I woke up ready for the first day of the rest of my life. I had the inspiration that would carry through my senior year. I had the confidence that I could accomplish anything I set my mind to. While many of my friends were enjoying their senior year, I was a man on a mission. I would finally bear down on my studies. Unlike many of my classmates, I would not touch any alcohol. I would be completely focused on my goals. This was the turning point. I listened to that tape every night to stay focused.

The start of my senior year was upon me. I had to focus not only on my studies but on staying healthy through my football season. I couldn't help looking back on the previous years. In my sophomore year, a broken right femur had ended my football season and canceled most of my hockey season at a critical time in a hockey player's development. I'd come back for my junior year and led our senior-laden football squad to a 7–2 record and gotten bumped just out of a state championship berth. During the hockey season, I'd led the team in scoring and helped us get to our second-straight state championship. I'd also been a starter on the baseball team.

I had a real fear of playing football, as our entire line had graduated. In my junior year, our offensive line averaged 230 pounds. In my senior year, they averaged less than 170 pounds. I weighed more than the typical lineman in front of me.

We were switching offenses to the wishbone in order to compensate for our undermanned team. I certainly did not want to get hurt again and miss my senior season of hockey. Breaking my femur was the most excruciating experience of my life. I did not want to go through that again. But I loved playing and had all my best friends on the team. So I needed to make the commitment and make it the greatest year of my life.

We got out to a fast start by knocking off Bishop Hendricken in a 22–21 comeback thriller. After that, we had numerous comeback victories against superior opponents. We were trailing at halftime in many of our games, but we always seemed to pull out a victory. We only had one loss the entire season, and that was against perennial state champion Rogers High School. We capped off the season with a fourth-straight win against our rival, Woonsocket High School, in the traditional Thanksgiving Day football game. I finished the season as the state's best passer and got a berth on the second team all-state team.

I also finished the first quarter with a 3.6 grade point average—by far the best average of my high school career. My parents were ecstatic.

Mission accomplished.

The day after Thanksgiving was the first practice of the hockey season. This was what I was waiting for. My dream was to play for a Division 1 program, make the Olympics, and play pro hockey.

I couldn't have been further from my goals at that moment.

The problem was that I was not in one of the better hockey programs in the state. We played in Division 4, and exposure to top programs would be a problem. Nobody took me or the lower divisions seriously. I knew I would need to go to prep school to get to a Division 1 school. I would also need to have an incredible year to make this happen. But I had faith and newfound inspiration that this would happen if I dedicated myself.

My senior year in hockey was a dream come true. I got out to a fast start by scoring five goals in my first game and never looked back. I had no mercy for my opponents. Until the coach sat me in games that were out of hand, I was relentless. I was not going to apologize to anyone. I desperately needed to make a statement.

I did have one pretty big failure that stood out during the season. I was invited to play in the Division 1 all-star game midway through the season. As the runaway scoring leader in the state, I was anxious to prove myself to everyone. I put a tremendous amount of pressure on myself in that game, and it didn't exactly help.

Playing against Rhode Island's best players, I was a little bit of a fish out of water. The game was two steps quicker than Division 4, so it took me most of the game to adjust to that speed of play. I ended up playing poorly.

It was the perfect performance for all the naysayers out there. It pissed me off that they thought I was a joke and could score only against lower-level talent. I heard everyone talking behind my back. It's a small state, and word gets around.

I used that moment not to destroy myself but to fuel my fire. I was determined to get the last laugh. I had faith that, given the time to develop, I could be as good as or better than everyone else out on that ice. I often told myself that I was the better athlete and that I needed to trust that it would eventually come out. It took many years, but that faith paid off.

I finished the year with a record 105 points in twenty-five games. I had fourteen multiple-goal games, seven hat tricks, three five-goal games, and one four-goal game. I averaged over two goals and four points a game. In five playoff games, I finished with twenty-one points.

The key to being a successful athlete is to be consistent and perform in the most important moments. This mindset ultimately came through for me in the toughest of circumstances and helped propel my career going forward.

We entered the state championship series as the underdog to Tolman High School. They were a deeper team than us and had shut us out twice in the regular season. They were cocky and overconfident but with good reason. They had effectively shut me and our entire offense down. To be honest, it was downright embarrassing.

We got out to an ugly start as they were up 4–0 late in the second period of game 1. They were outplaying us again and outshot us by a wide margin. I was getting very frustrated, as they were all over me. The pressure was at an all-time high. Finally, with a few minutes to play in the second period, we finally broke the ice and made it 4–1. They struck back quickly and restored their four-goal cushion to make it 5–1 at the end of two periods.

The break between periods couldn't have come at a better time for me and the entire team. Having one period left and being down four goals to a team that had pretty much dominated us the entire season could have been a good thing in a weird way. It made us focus on the process and not the outcome. Nobody said it, but no one expected us to come back and win. We just wanted to score the next goal. That was it.

I had to refocus myself. The game couldn't have gone worse for me. Being shut out for eight straight periods when I averaged over a point per period was humbling. I was worrying about all the wrong things. What would people say around the state if I didn't help us win? What would they say at school? My dad's coworkers were at the game. He had been bragging about me, I'm sure. I was too focused on scoring goals, and that definitely wasn't helping me.

Reaching back into my memory bank, I found some inspiration. Of course, I thought of the Cranston East game. What did I do then that made me so dominant? I'd had complete moment-to-moment focus. I hadn't been worried about the outcome of that game. I'd taken it just one play at a time.

Right then, I decided to just dominate my next shift. I wasn't going to worry about anything else but that. They would have to kill me to get the puck off my stick in the next shift. It was now or never.

I came out in the third period absolutely possessed. One shift at a time, I dominated. We came out and quickly scored two goals. I had finally broken the drought and registered two assists. Momentum had definitely shifted. With about six minutes to play, we scored again and cut it to 5–4.

This is when the impossible happened. With about three minutes to play, I was skating down the left side and, just before crossing the goal line, slid a backhand past their goalie to tie the game 5–5. The packed arena at Brown University was going crazy.

With about two minutes to play, I stole a puck just inside their blue line, faked out a couple of defenders, and picked the top corner to put us up 6–5. We were absolutely dominating them, and they were stunned. To their credit, they came back thirty seconds later and tied the game at 6–6.

What came next was another out-of-body experience. The packed house was deafening. With seconds left in the game, I raced down the ice with the puck and stopped behind the left side of their net. I looked up and noticed that there were only a few seconds left on the clock. I saw an opening on the other side of the net and, out of desperation, wrapped the puck around the net and scored with one second left.

Everyone went crazy. It was the most dramatic and amazing victory I had ever been a part of. We'd been down 5–1 in the final fifteen minutes against a team that had shut us out in two regular-season games and was showing no signs of changing the tides.

There is a lot to learn from that game.

I still use this moment to convince myself that I am capable of accomplishing great things. It takes up a big space in my memory bank. I wish everyone had the ability to feel this moment. I felt that I was a man of destiny.

Unfortunately, we lost Game 2 of the championship series, and it set up a winner-take-all in Game 3. It was time to put Game 1 and Game 2 behind me and focus on the task at hand. I wanted to finish up my high school career with another championship and have another game of my life.

In front of a packed house, we got out to a fast start and never looked back. We pulled out a 7–5 victory. I finished with four goals and two assists in the deciding game. Finishing the series with seven goals and five assists, I was named the most valuable player of the state tournament. It capped an unforgettable senior year, but it hadn't been without its disappointments.

I finished the season as the state's leading scorer. I was awarded Hockey Night in Boston's, Rhode Island Player of the Year and received the Willam H. Thayer Award as the outstanding hockey player for the interscholastic season.

However, I was not selected as one of the top fifteen players in Rhode Island that year. I was left off the most prestigious all-state teams. And I did not make first, second, or honorable mention teams in 1989. No question, this put more fuel in my tank. But I also was realistic. To be honest, many of the other players were better than me. I took the slight as an opportunity to self-evaluate. I had a lot of work to do, but I was inspired to stick with it.

I'd set the bar high for myself both academically and athletically. And I'd achieved a lot of my goals but not all of them. Still, I accomplished way more than I would have if I set the bar lower.

If you are keeping score at home, here are the results:

1) Win a state championship in football. NO
2) Be the first team all-state quarterback. NO
3) Win a state championship in hockey. YES
4) Average three goals a game. NO
5) Be all-state in hockey. NO
6) Don't be another "Joe Smith." YES

I'd gone into the year with the hopes and fears of becoming a high school legend. To clarify, I wanted to be a high school legend, but I did not want that to define me for the rest of my life.

I had much bigger goals in mind.

Chapter 3
Cushing Academy

"Life is inherently risky. There is only one big risk
you should avoid at all cost, and that is the risk
of doing nothing."
–Denis Waitley

After graduating from high school, I decided to enroll as a postgraduate at Cushing Academy. Essentially, I was repeating my senior year. I did this for two reasons: to improve my grades and SAT score and to get a Division 1 scholarship to college. I wanted more than anything to compete at the highest level in college in hopes of becoming a professional athlete.

This was an easy but unbelievably tough decision. All my friends were going off to college, where they would experience their first taste of freedom. Thankfully, my parents had the means and support to allow me to chase my dreams. This went on to be the most difficult, but without question, best decision of my life.

I was putting in all my chips by entering prep school to chase my lifelong dreams. There was no going back. And it wasn't going to be easy, what with Friday-night study halls, Saturday classes, and occasionally Saturday-night detention. While all my friends were out partying and having fun, I was locked into repeating my senior year in hopes of achieving my dreams. I didn't want to fail in my quest and did want to prove all the naysayers wrong.

I had been one of the best hockey players in the state up until I entered high school. When my parents decided not to send me to one of the elite hockey programs in the state, I quickly fell behind my peers. It was a struggle throughout high school to see players I was better than get the recognition I craved. In fact, I was not chosen as one of the best fifteen players despite setting a record for scoring in my senior year. And I lived in the country's smallest state. This slap in the face was my driving force. It fueled my desire through the toughest year of my life.

I was planning on just concentrating on playing hockey but quickly realized after my entrance interview that the football team needed a quarterback. It wasn't outright said but insinuated that I would have a better chance of getting in if I decided to also play football. Looking back on it, I was Brendan Fraser's character in *School Ties*. I felt they were using me for football, and I was going to use them to get a Division 1 hockey scholarship and get drafted into the NHL.

At the start of football season, all I wanted to do was stay healthy and finish the season. It was a completely different atmosphere than high school, but it still fostered the same type of teammates. Coming in as a postgraduate who was there mainly for hockey, I had many skeptics—one being an assistant football coach who also held a high position in the school administration.

This coach felt he needed to challenge me during camp by sending certain players to intentionally hit me. This was not common practice for a football team. Quarterbacks were always off-limits in practice in order to save them from getting injured. Our head coach did not do anything to stop it. I can only assume that because of the assistant coach's position at the school, nobody—including the coaching staff—wanted to risk getting on his bad side. This sort of thing never happened at a public high school, and I was pissed off.

As practice went on, I purposely went out of my way to run the ball straight at the defense. I would try anything I could to run over and hurt anyone getting in my way. More than once, I slammed the ball down after a play and smiled at the assistant coach. This was the beginning of our not-so-pleasant relationship.

As the football season started, his attitude toward me began to change. I got the crap kicked out of me in our first game but led our team on multiple scoring drives. We ended up winning that game, and he suddenly respected me. This just drove me to prove more people wrong.

During the season, the athletic director called me into his office and asked me about my intentions regarding college. He told me he had many Division 1AA schools that had reached out to him about my aspirations of playing college football. I was conflicted because I loved football and my teammates. But ultimately, my goals were to play college and pro hockey. I didn't want to regret not fulfilling that mission. I told him thanks but no thanks.

While I was playing football, I was also well aware that most of my fellow hockey players were preparing for the upcoming season. I knew I had to do more on my own to prepare outside of just playing football. At night, I would do push-ups to exhaustion with my roommate, Nate. I would also get up early in the morning a few days a week to go running.

We were not allowed out of our dorms until six a.m., but I would sneak out before that, when it was still dark. I got up one morning, feeling exhausted. I struggled to get going. I contemplated going back to bed, but forced myself to go running anyway. I was getting up because nobody else was.

It was darker than usual that day. I didn't think too much of it until I got back to my dorm room.

As I was lying back in bed, I noticed my roommate shaking. I thought this was odd until I heard him laughing. That was when I realized that he and a bunch of the guys in the dorm had changed my clock after I went to bed the night before. I must have looked like a crazy person running around the track at two a.m.! But it was the dedication I needed to keep up and gain a mental edge on my competition.

I stepped on the ice for the first time that year in late November, the day after the football season ended. I was far behind most of my hockey teammates, as I was the only one who played football.

Playing hockey at the prep school level was a big adjustment for me, what with the speed of the game, the new systems, and the new teammates. If there was one thing I could always do, it was score goals. I just needed time for my skating to catch up to the competition. My solution was to use my physical abilities and hit everything that moved on the ice. I was also lucky enough to be linemates with future Olympian John Lilley.

Early on in the season, our coach, Steve Jacobs, was responsible for the biggest improvement in my game almost instantly. I was in need of new skates, and had asked my father to buy me a new pair. He was not crazy about spending money on equipment. I guess I can't blame him because he was raising five kids, three of whom were in college at the same time. Up to that point, I'd only had brand-new skates twice in my life. Since most of my skates had been hand-me-downs, when I got a new pair, I was petrified to grow out of them. As a result, my father always bought my skates bigger so I could grow into them. The only problem was that my feet stopped growing before the rest of my body did. So when my dad bought me the new Micron skates, he bought a size nine, just like the ones I had used for the last three years.

As I was putting on my new skates on in the locker room before practice, my coach looked over and asked me a life-changing question: "Mike, what size skates are those?"

"Size nine," I said.

"What size shoe are you?"

"Size nine. Why?"

"You do know that skates run two sizes smaller, don't you?" he said.

Um, no. I didn't. I had been wearing skates that were two sizes too big for me during my entire high school career. Think about playing any sport in shoes that were two sizes bigger than your feet. It's the equivalent of wearing clown shoes or flippers in a sporting event.

As soon as I wore skates the right size for me, my skating dramatically improved. I was quicker and could turn and cross over better. It is kind of laughable that I hadn't realized how poorly my skates fit. Fixing that helped me improve rapidly that season. I'd always been able to score, but now I could keep up with the pace of the game.

The defining game for me that season was against Culver Military Academy. The game took place during the Christmas break, and many major colleges and pro scouts attended it. Ironically, I was feeling a little bit under the weather that day. A former football teammate of mine from high school had come up with me to the game. He was home on his college break and was probably coming off a ten-day bender.

Knowing it was a huge game, I came out with a little bit more energy. I ended up having two goals with a few assists and laid out five or six of my opponents. It was one of those games in which I felt I had finally put my name on the map.

It also reinforced for me the power of moment-to-moment focus. I felt so lousy that all I could do was think about the shift I was on. Staying in the moment unleashed a tremendous amount of energy and made the game easy to play. This is a theme that I later realized is a critical factor in performing at a high level in games.

After the game, my coach told me a few NHL scouts wanted to talk to me. As I came out of the locker room, I was approached by scouts from Calgary, the New York Rangers, and the Minnesota North Stars. They asked if I had time to grab a quick bite to eat down the street at a local diner. I explained I had a friend in town and asked if it was okay for him to tag along with me. They said it was no problem.

I was in a state of disbelief as I approached my car, where my friend was waiting. I got in, looked at him, and said, "Could you believe that?"

He looked at me in a state of shock and replied, "What?"

"I just had the greatest game of my life, and you are here to witness it."

Still looking at me, he seemed embarrassed and then confessed, "I actually slept through your whole game."

"Well," I told him, "we are going out to eat with some NHL scouts because I just put myself on the map."

It's funny to look back on it and think that my best friend from home was too hungover to witness the hockey game that ended up getting me drafted into the NHL.

Shortly after the game against Culver Military Academy, things started to change. I had been getting a lot of Division 3 interest, but now I was getting some Division 1 looks. In fact, a high-level Division 3 school had been at the Culver game and informed my coach that they were no longer interested in me. The coach pulled me aside and said, "The bad news is they are not recruiting you anymore. But the good news is that's because you are definitely going Division 1."

Schools like Boston College, the University of New Hampshire, and Providence College started showing interest in me. Eventually, Boston College and New Hampshire offered me the opportunity to walk onto their teams. Providence was my hometown team and my number-one choice. They had one scholarship left when they saw me in a tournament at Tabor Academy. I had a couple of goals in that particular game but was told that Providence offered the scholarship to another player right after the game. It was a pretty big blow.

The one school that showed the most interest in me was Saint Anselm College, a Division 3 school. That would end up being my one and only official college visit. They offered me a 90 percent scholarship, and it was nice to see how much they wanted me. I loved the coaching staff, and one of my best friends was attending. The only problem was that it was not Division 1.

The University of Lowell in Massachusetts showed interest late in the season. I didn't know a lot about them, and quite frankly, I didn't care. They were Division 1, and that was my goal. I didn't even go on an official overnight visit like every other serious recruit. I went in for a day visit, and they offered me a quarter scholarship. It was the equivalent of a meal plan. No guarantees—just the chance to realize one of my lifelong goals. I signed my letter of intent shortly thereafter.

At the end of the season, I finished as Cushing Academy's second-leading scorer behind John Lilley. We ended up losing in the quarterfinals to Canterbury Prep, and I moved on to baseball season. This closed out playing five seasons each of football, hockey, and baseball between high school and prep school.

I turned nineteen in April and had not concentrated on one sport yet. The lessons I learned through these seasons served me well as I climbed the ladder in hockey. The most important one was learning how to fail and then improve.

I trusted myself as an athlete first and a player in the particular sport second. I knew how to work hard to overcome weakness and turn it into power. There is no question that one sport helped the other. I was tough and resilient. As I went into college, I was still improving while my competition was stagnating.

At the school's end-of-the-year banquet, I was awarded the Betty Davis award as the best all-around athlete at Cushing Academy, as well as the MVP of the football team. It was a tough year, but it was easily the best decision I'd made to that point. I was one step closer to my dreams of playing Division 1 hockey and potentially getting into the pros. I would never have had the opportunities in the next ten years and beyond if it hadn't been for Cushing Academy.

Chapter 4
The NHL Draft

"Great moments are born from great opportunity."
—Herb Brooks

I returned home in early June after graduating from Cushing Academy and was, for the moment, satisfied with what I had accomplished that year. I went to work on a training program that my high school football coach gave me. I knew that the end of the month could potentially change my life.

That's because the NHL draft was coming up at the end of June. I knew I was a long shot at best to be drafted. I was excited at the prospect and confident that I'd done everything I could to put myself in this position. If I didn't get drafted, there was no doubt I would be disappointed. I had given it my all in the last year. But no matter what happened, I had no regrets and would have peace of mind.

True to everything I've ever done, I kept the prospects of the NHL draft a secret to everyone but my parents. I instead tried to focus on the task at hand. I needed to put in my daily work to have a successful start to my college career.

The anxiety built throughout the month, and I did my best to distract myself. There are few times in anyone's life when a single moment can change everything. That day for me had finally arrived.

It was June 20, 1990, and I was waiting for the 1990 NHL draft to start. I was not on the NHL Central Scouting Bureau (CSS) list of top prospects in the world. The CSS is a department within the National Hockey League that ranks prospects for the NHL entry draft at specific times during the hockey season. Players are ranked based on how well they will translate to the professional game. It was founded by hockey executive Jack Button in 1975 to establish a centralized database of NHL prospects.

Basically, if you are not listed, then it is very unlikely that you could get drafted. I, however, had caught the eye of some NHL scouts due to my strong postgraduate year. It was the first year that I had played with the elite players in the country, and I had adapted well. I was a raw talent in hockey and had gained more interest because I was a multisport athlete.

Fortunately, Lowell had offered me a small Division 1 scholarship to play hockey, and I'd accepted. They wanted a physical athlete who could develop into a top hockey player. They took a chance on me. However, it was unlikely that I would be chosen in the draft.

The night before the draft, I did reveal to John, my closest friend, the possibility of being drafted. He was the only person I confided in besides my parents. I didn't tell anyone because

I didn't want to jinx myself. Having to explain to people that I didn't get drafted was not ideal. I would rather surprise people if I did.

The day started early for me, and I was able to get in a workout before the draft started. The draft was held in Vancouver, British Columbia, and started at noon EST. The first round was televised on national TV and lasted about two hours.

The nerves I felt throughout the day were indescribable. I paced around my house and tried to calculate how long the draft would last. I was interrupted only by John, who was calling every hour from work to check in. Minute by minute and hour by hour, I stressed over the thought of not being drafted.

I was on the cusp of accomplishing a dream that, a year earlier, seemed almost impossible. I wanted to prove to everyone who doubted me that I had the ability to be a world-class athlete. More importantly, I wanted to prove to myself that all the hard work and suffering I'd gone through to get to that moment had been worth it.

As it approached seven p.m., it appeared that I wasn't going to be drafted by an NHL team. John had just finished work, and, with his parents away, I decided to go drown my sorrows at his house. I told my parents that if anyone called, they could reach me at John's place.

This was before the days of the internet, and it was impossible to see if the draft was still going on. My best guess was that it was over. I'll admit that I was crushed. I went over to John's house, and we sat and watched TV at his kitchen table. We didn't say anything to each other, and he didn't pry because he knew how much the draft had meant to me. We sat for about an hour (which seemed like an eternity) and watched meaningless shows.

Then the phone rang, and we just stared at each other.

John jumped up and answered it. I can still remember the stunned look on his face when he realized it was my father. There was only one reason my dad would call. John started jumping up and down and passed me the phone.

"Hey, Dad . . . " I said.

"You did it!" he told me.

"What?"

"You did it!"

The only thing I could say was "If you are kidding, I will never talk to you again." Meanwhile, John was jumping up and down screaming.

"The Calgary Flames just drafted you in the ninth round," my dad said.

Instantly, my life changed forever.

I really do wish everyone could experience that feeling. To accomplish a major part of my dream and now be part of a professional franchise was incredible. A year earlier, I hadn't been considered one of the top fifteen players in my state. Now I was considered the 188th best prospect in the world. It validated my year in prep school, the hard work, and the mental stress I had put on myself.

John and I immediately jumped in the car and headed to my parents' house. The ride seemed like a blur. We were both still astonished at the news. When I walked in the door, my parents had huge smiles on their faces. I gave them both big hugs. They were as stunned as I was. My parents' best friends, the Lynches, showed up, and we told them the news. Then my brother Kevin and his friend came by, and we shared the news with them.

Nobody around me had known that the NHL draft was even that day, never mind that I might be chosen. My father kept handing me and my brother money to enjoy the night. He called everyone he knew, from siblings to relatives to friends. A carload of girlfriends stopped by, and I ran out to tell them. They were all stunned.

We decided to go over to John's and celebrate. My brother took all the money and ran out to the liquor store. I knew this would surely turn out to be a big party. When we got to John's house, I called my high school girlfriend at work and told her the news that I'd been drafted. She asked, "By who? The army? The navy?" She told the girls at work, and nobody believed that someone who played at Cumberland could get drafted. "That only happens to players at the Mount!" they said.

My brother and more friends came by to celebrate with me. It was easily the greatest day of my life. We partied throughout the night and well into the morning. The first thing a friend said to me was "No matter what else you do in your life, you can say that you were drafted in the NHL."

Well, if I could accomplish this first step, I had bigger things in mind. I was now on a mission!

NHL draft picks of note in the 1990 NHL draft were Jaromír Jágr, Owen Nolan, Martin Brodeur, and Sergei Zubov. My college roommate, Travis Tucker, was taken four spots after me in the tenth round by the Detroit Red Wings. So I have that over him, which is nice.

The mission started right away. Time was running out to prepare for my upcoming freshmen season at Lowell. I was well aware that I was the last recruit to commit to the school and had the smallest scholarship they could offer. I really didn't care because all I wanted was a chance.

I needed to maximize every day and decided that crushing the preseason testing was the only thing I could control. I formulated a plan and then executed on it. Every hour of every day was accounted for. Specific workouts, work, eating, sleeping, and hanging out with friends were all on the schedule.

Three days on and one day off was the regimen throughout the summer. After waking around seven a.m. and having breakfast, I would start no later than eight a.m. with a run or bike ride, then I'd jump rope.

At ten a.m., I would spend the next two hours on a daily rotation of legs or upper-body exercises. I would eat from noon to one p.m., then go off to work as a lifeguard from one to five p.m.

I ate from five to six p.m. Then I would put in an hour of shooting pucks followed by an hour of working out. It was always some combination of boxing, karate, swimming, cross-country skiing, or running hills. To be honest, it was a lot easier than it looks. I would just focus on one day at a time. Yesterday is history, tomorrow is a mystery, and today is a gift—and that's why they call it the present.

Having a schedule like this relieved stress and kept me focused every day. I took it one day at a time, stacking days, until I left for school. There were only twenty-four hours in a day, and I decided to maximize them.

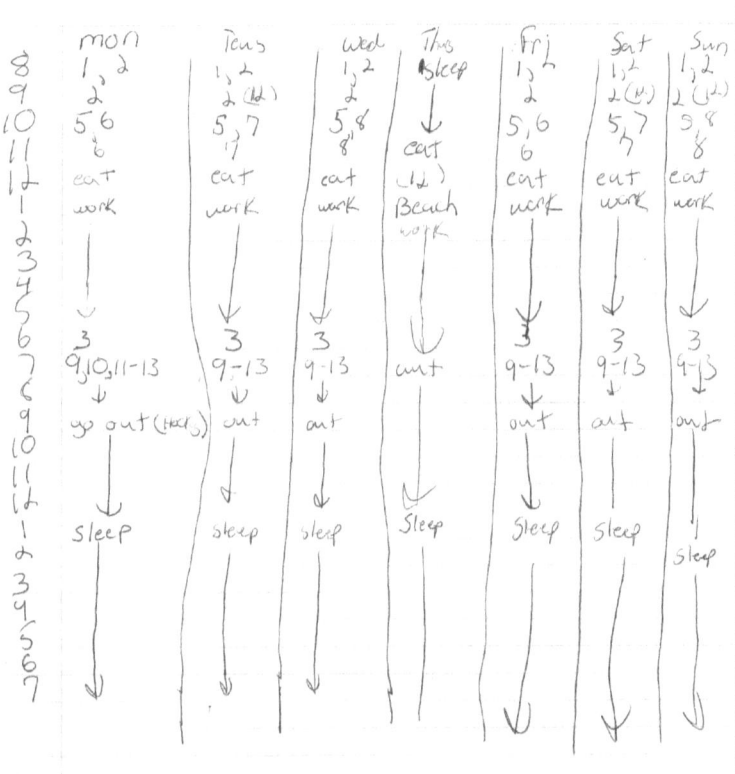

Workout Sample

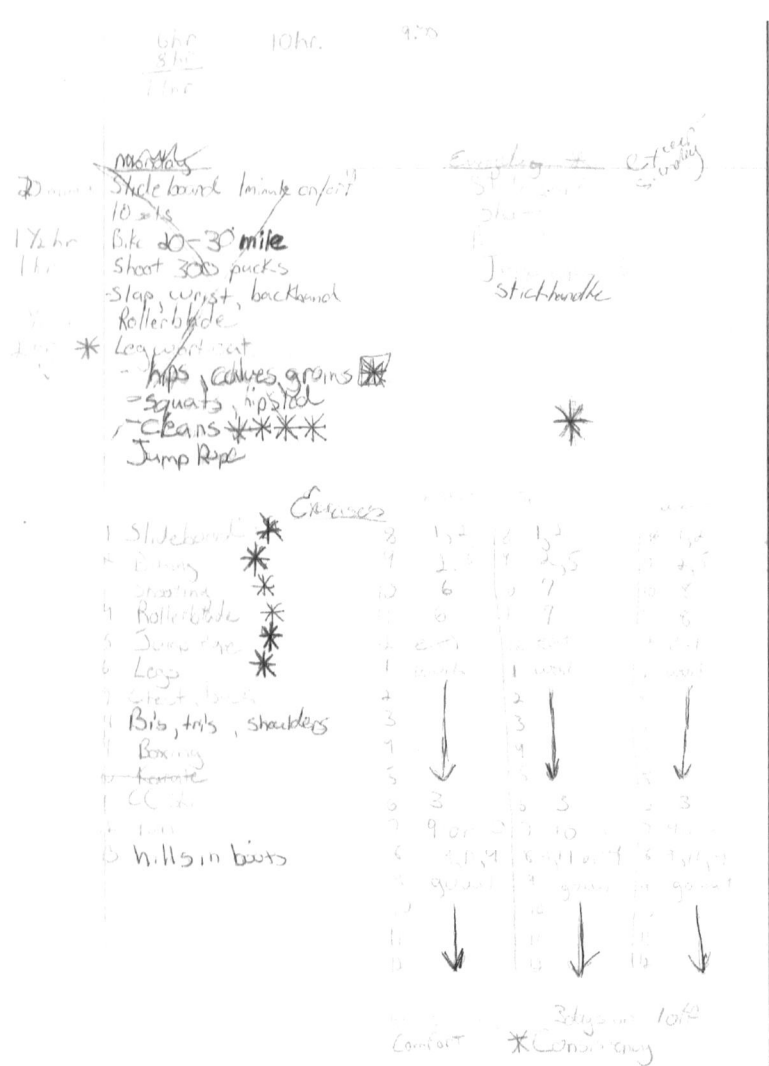

Nowadays, there are many ways to make your own schedule. Use apps on your device, schedule it on your phone calendar, or, my personal favorite, make a simple pen-and-paper schedule. There is no doubt in my mind that this set me up for the success that I went on to have in the future. I was able to work out extremely hard and enjoy my time with friends and family due to that schedule. When motivation started to wane, I would listen to my tape and refocus myself. The commitment was always there. But sometimes, I needed the extra boost. I could always count on that tape.

And I was always curious about how I could get better—slide board, biking, jumping rope, running hills in boots, boxing, karate, rollerblading, shooting, eye exercises, juggling, etc. Whatever I could find, short of doing anything illegal, I would try. This led me to focus on the mental side of the game long before most players did.

There is no doubt that I was blessed to get drafted. It was a huge moment in my life. From that point going forward, I was on a mission to do everything I could to make it to the NHL. If that didn't happen, it would be disappointing. But I could live with that. I was determined to live with no regrets and do everything I could to make it.

With all that work done, I was ready to make my mark once I started school.

Chapter 5
Lowell

T he summer leading to my freshman year, I worked out like crazy. I took my high school football training program and faithfully followed it. The only problem was that it wasn't specific to hockey. Nonetheless, I worked out and skated as much as I could.

I came into my freshman year relatively unknown. Even though I was drafted that summer, most people didn't know who I was. Hockey is a small world, and most elite players knew each other because they either played against each other or had played on all-star teams over the years.

I knew I had to make an impact right away to get some attention from the coaching staff. I was the last of six recruits to commit to the school, and they'd barely given me a scholarship. To reduce my tuition, the coaching staff convinced me to have criminal justice as a major. That allowed me to get in-state tuition because my home state of Rhode Island did not offer that major in any of its state universities. It was a nice loophole that resulted in significant savings. Even though I wanted to major in a different subject, the opportunity was too good to pass up.

The first team activity didn't take place until a week into school. My housing was screwed up, and I was put into a dorm room with a guy from the wrestling team. All my fellow hockey freshmen were in another dorm and spent the first week of school bonding and hanging out. So I was kind of an outsider when we gathered as a team for the first time.

I'm not sure if any of them realized I was part of the freshman class when we had to test in the weight room on that first day. I wasn't the biggest guy in the class and didn't look like the strongest either. That perception quickly changed when I was tested on the bench press.

Everyone was tested for max bench press and max squat. It was a small weight room (embarrassing for a Division 1 team), and about thirty guys crammed into the room. The whole team was screaming for anyone who was maxing out.

When my time came at the end to bench press, there was an upperclassman who had already broken and set the record at 315 pounds. Nobody else even came close. This was my time to make my mark.

I did a quick warm-up at 225 and then quickly moved up to 275. The trainer asked me if I was confident that I could lift it. What he didn't know was that I'd been lifting 275 for ten reps at the end of the summer. I put it up without a struggle.

Then I moved to 300 pounds and started to get the attention of the coaching staff and other players. Three hundred pounds went up without a problem, and the place went crazy. I asked what the record was and was told it was 315. I asked them to put 315 pounds on, and the whole place stopped to watch my lift. They went crazy again when 315 went up pretty easily.

The trainer asked me if I wanted to continue. Without hesitation, I said, "Put 330 on the bar." I figured if I was going to break the record, then I should smash it. I could definitely feel the jealousy from the previous record holder and everyone else's astonishment. I didn't look like I could lift half that weight. At six one and 187 pounds, I was a good size for a hockey player, but I certainly didn't look like I was that strong.

As I paced around the room, waiting to attempt the 330 pounds, the crowd started getting louder and louder. I positioned myself on the bench and hoisted the weight off the bar. With everything I had, I brought it to my chest and exploded up. I struggled to get the weight up but finally completed the lift. The place went crazy. I'd just welcomed myself to the team. I guess a few people now knew me.

I believe that accomplishing this feat was a huge reason for my later success. It bought me credibility. Plus, the coaching staff witnessed my feat. I think that, as a result, they were willing to give me the time to develop at a critical time in my career.

The start of my freshmen year got off to a tough start because I broke my hand in the first exhibition game. Although

I didn't miss any games, I did have to play with a cast for the first month. I was a steady fourth-line player for much of the first half of the season. I did anything I could to stay in the lineup. My game at that time was very physical. I was referred to as a grinder. The coaching staff and, most importantly, Bill Riley, the head coach, rewarded me for my efforts with much-needed playing time.

My skating continued to improve throughout the year, and I was getting more and more offensive opportunities. I was growing more confident every game and started to get some special team time. The coaching staff's rewarded playing time started to pay off. I ended up producing five goals and eight assists for thirteen points. It was a solid freshman year, and, more importantly, I gained a ton of confidence by playing every game and a regular shift.

One big moment that stuck with the rest of my life was a game that we played at the University of New Hampshire. We had a senior, who never talked much, get up before the game and give a speech. It probably went in one ear and out the other to most of the players in the room. He got emotional as he started to talk about how quickly time in college goes. He said it seemed like yesterday that he was a freshman and that we should not take this time for granted. I often thought about that moment for the rest of my career and tried to not take it for granted. As an adult, I talk about it often with the kids that I coach. The most successful people understand this concept.

We did not have a very good team, and we finished with eight wins for the season. The program was in turmoil due to NCAA violations committed over the previous few years and the resulting probation. This was long before most of the players on the team had arrived on campus, but it was going to cast a black cloud on the university's program and make us a laughingstock across the country.

We were the only Division 1 sport on the campus, and fellow athletes and students already didn't like us. Included among them was my future wife, who was the star of the tennis team. Many of our players were thinking about transferring. The only problem was that most players, including me, had nowhere else to go. I was very unsure about my future with the program. But that all changed with one quick conversation.

Before the end of the year, our new coach, Bruce Crowder, came up to me in the cafeteria and wanted to chat for a bit. He ended up telling me that he thought that I could be a top player in Hockey East. He said that if I continued to work hard, I had a lot of potential. The crazy thing was that I was just hoping to have the opportunity to compete for a roster spot the next year.

It is funny how I can look back at moments in my life and realize that this one brief conversation catapulted me into a national story that helped change the image of the program.

Sophomore Year

The summer before my sophomore year, I spent three weeks in Brainerd, Minnesota, training with a bunch of NHL prospects. I trained with a number of American Hockey League (AHL) players and fellow college players. It was the exposure and work that I needed to improve my game.

We would be on the ice twice a day and have one off-ice workout per day. It was a grind, but seeing how professionals and top college players prepare was beneficial. I could evaluate what I needed to improve on to be able to compete at the top level.

Skating was my challenge due to my limited time spent on the ice through high school, and this was the exact training I needed to make a big jump in my game. Speed and quickness in the way they played the game were necessities.

When I returned home from Brainerd, I understood how to get better. I took that knowledge and self-evaluation and went to work on it. Much like every other summer, I continued to put the work in. I would continue to implement different training strategies to work on those weaknesses. Platform plyometric shoes, slide board training, and off-ice exercises I learned at the camp. Whatever I could do to improve, I did.

My overall game was evolving through all my training. I was building confidence from the training and the words that Coach Crowder gave me in the cafeteria. I was ready to take the next step.

Coach Crowder also said a few words to me in front of the team before school ended that motivated me for preseason testing. In our team meeting, he said, "Mike Murray can bench press the gym, but he needs to wear sweatpants at the beach." He meant that even though I broke the bench press record, I tested only average for squats. I could have whined about the comment, but I decided to use it as motivation.

Strong legs are critical for success in hockey. I never knew how to do squats and learned how to train only through my high school football program. I was new to training specifically for hockey. He was right, and I realized that I needed to focus even more on leg strength that summer.

As soon as we got back to school, we did our preseason testing. I ended up equaling my bench press record. Then came the squat testing. As you might guess, I went on to break the squat record. Nowadays, these are probably outdated tests. But back then, it was the only thing we could measure ourselves by.

You can't fake the bench press, and you can't fake squats. You either put in the work, or you don't. **"There are plenty of things you can't control, and that's why it is critical to focus on what you can control."** It was the edge that I needed, and the coaches took notice. They are more willing to take time with a player who proves they work hard.

As we started training camp in early October, I was putting a tremendous amount of pressure on myself. But I was not performing up to my or the coaches' expectations. A week into camp, the coach brought me into his office and asked me what the problem was. I didn't have an answer for him. He said, "Maybe I was wrong about you."

Well, that was pretty crushing.

As luck would have it, we had a scheduled day off over that weekend. I decided to go home for the night and decompress. I had put in all that work, and everything seemed to be falling apart. Maybe I wasn't good enough. Maybe I did not belong. I had a fleeting thought of leaving school.

I did a lot of thinking that night and came to the revelation that I was worried about all the things I couldn't control. What would my friends think? What would all the people from home think? Were all the so-called experts right about me?

That night, I decided I was going to stop worrying about everything and just focus on the next practice. Every time it was my turn in a drill, I would dominate. If I had the puck, they would have to kill me to get it away from me. There was no quit in me. This was it.

That little wake-up call from the coach actually let me reset myself. I knew I had put in all the work and that I'd left no stone unturned. That was when I learned to trust the process. To trust all the work I'd put in that summer and let the results come.

Almost immediately, my game started to change. The very next practice, I was named practice player of the day. I proceeded to dominate in practice one day at a time. A huge weight was lifted off me.

This new mindset catapulted me into the exhibition game against Acadia University out of Canada. We beat them, and I was able to break the ice and score two goals. The perfect remedy for confidence for me was what I was accustomed to doing my entire hockey career—scoring. I got on a roll from that game that few players had ever achieved before. Or achieved since.

The first game of the regular season was against the University of Alabama in Huntsville, and I scored another two goals. Then came an early season tournament—USAir Classic—

hosted by Providence College. They were one of the top-ranked teams in the country and a team I was not very fond of. The main reason: I grew up a Providence College fan and would have loved to have played for them. But they hadn't recruited me. Now my mission was to destroy them every time we played.

We opened up against Elmira University, and I scored a hat trick (three goals). I was full of confidence heading into the championship game against Providence College, even though they were heavily favored. The crowd was packed with a lot of my family and friends. I am sure many people were there to see if I was really any good.

We ended up upsetting them. I scored the game-winning goal and was named the MVP of the USAir Classic. It was a surreal experience to be hoisting that trophy after what I had been through in the last few years.

I started to receive a lot of attention around the league and even from the local papers in Rhode Island. I believe people were perplexed that I could come out of Cumberland, where nobody recruited me, and be dominant at the Division 1 level. I had eight goals in our first four games. To be honest, I was a little surprised.

It only escalated from there.

We were winning hockey games, and I had scored seventeen goals in the first ten games of the season. There seemed to be a big buzz around school, what with a new coach and the national headlines I was receiving. I was featured in local papers and between periods on televised games. I was also the subject of a featured article in *College Hockey Magazine*. It was the attention our program needed after getting so much negative attention the previous year.

The attention was a little overwhelming. My freshman year, I'd been just trying to make the lineup every night. Now I was the focal point of the opposing team's game plan. I reached twenty goals faster (in seventeen games) than any other player in Lowell history.

By the time Christmas rolled around, I was getting mugged by every team in the league. Halfway through the season, I was leading the country in goal scoring. I was at the top in goals per game and power-play goals.

My confidence was through the roof, and it showed on the ice. I was a little of an oddity, as I was a power forward playing at center. I played a very physical game and had good enough hands to score a lot of goals.

Murray skates to top echelon in Hockey East

By JIM SALISBURY
Times sports writer

CUMBERLAND — When he was racking up all those points a few winters ago at Cumberland High, the doubters, unimpressed with the caliber of his competition, would often sniff, "Yeah, but look who he's doing it against."

True, Mike Murray didn't play in the most respected high school hockey league in Rhode Island, and even 76 points in 20 games weren't enough to win over all the doubters.

"I heard it all the time," recalled Murray, who's gone on to UMass-Lowell and currently is the leading goal scorer in Hockey East with 21 goals in 20 games.

"Everyone said there was no way a guy playing Division Four high school hockey could play Division One in college. People doubted I could play

> "Very few walk-ons do what he's doing."
>
> — Lowell coach
> Bruce Crowder

COLLEGE recruiters didn't come in waves to Murray's front door, so off he went to Cushing Academy in Ashburnham, Mass. for a year of prep school. At Cushing, he again set the nets ablaze with 27 goals and 28 assists in 21 games.

Now the recruiters would storm in, right?

Not really. The storm was more like a sprinkle.

The downfall that year was when I separated my shoulder at the beginning of a game against Merrimack College. A typical play that I did a hundred times was going in and taking the defensemen's body at their blue line. The only problem this time was that I stepped on his stick and fell awkwardly into the boards. I received a concussion, and when I woke in the training room, I realized that I had separated my shoulder. It knocked me out of action for two weeks, and when I came back, all my strength was gone.

The edge to my game came from my strength. I was never the best skater, so I had to rely on my ability to make room for myself. Separating my shoulder took that edge from me. I struggled through the last eight to ten games of the season and ended up with a team-best twenty-four goals.

At the end of the season, I was awarded the Paul Hines Award as the Most Improved Player in New England and finished as our team's leading scorer and team MVP.

All in all, the year was a tremendous success. I had moved from a relatively unknown player to someone who was in the national spotlight. It is crazy to think that my season and career were almost over before they really even started.

Summer Leading Into Junior Year

I was getting interest from Team USA's national program. They invited me to their two-week training camp in Cromwell, Connecticut, over the summer. It was the jumping-off point for the 1994 Olympic team. It was a dream come true to participate in that camp.

It was also an amazing experience. Even though my dream was to play in the Olympics and represent my country, my game was more suited for the NHL than it was for the international game. I was a power forward and built my game more on strength than on speed. Olympics hockey was played on a bigger ice sheet than I was accustomed to playing on in North America. It required the team to emphasize speed over power.

However, the camp gave me a chance to show what I was capable of against the top talent in the US. I was at a big disadvantage because most of the players had already been in the junior US program, and I was still an unknown. It was funny that at the beginning of camp, each of us had to get up and tell what school we were playing at. The University of Lowell had just changed its name to the University of Massachusetts at Lowell (UMass Lowell), and when I introduced myself, no one had ever heard of it. My school had been down in the dumps for a number of years, and changing the name didn't help our recognition. Plus, being on probation the previous year made us a laughingstock in these circles. I was out to change this perception.

The camp was a two-week tryout that ended each week with an intrasquad game. At the end of the second week, they were going to pick a team that would travel to Finland for three weeks to play in a multination tournament. They were also picking a team later for the USA Cup to be played during the Christmas break.

It was clear that everyone wanted to be picked for the Finland team. The majority of the 1994 Olympic team would be picked from that team. We would have the exposure to and the opportunity to develop our skills on the international rinks for three weeks. It was, without question, my goal to make that team.

The training was very tough and competitive, with two-a-day skates and off-ice workouts. Everyone was trying their best to impress the coaching staff for a chance to make the national team. Each individual week would culminate with a game attended by all NHL scouts, agents, and college coaches.

I was on a line with two players from the University of Minnesota who went on to make the 1994 team—Darby Hendrickson and Craig Johnson. In the first game, I had two goals and an assist, and I led the game in scoring. It was the standout performance I needed to be in contention to make the team.

Many scouts and agents approached me and my father after the game. One of the scouts commented to my dad that I was on track to sign a million-dollar contract. I was the talk of the camp, and my play improved through the next week. I had another solid game the next week and ended up being one of the top scorers at the camp. I was pretty sure I had done everything I could to make the team. No regrets.

After the final game, we took a bus back to the hotel where they were going to announce the team for the Finland trip. I was sitting with a bunch of players on the bus, and they were discussing who they thought would make the trip. I remained quiet when one player from Boston University, whom I didn't particularly like, turned and said to me in front of everyone, "Well, you obviously made the team." I didn't really know what to say and just shrugged. I knew I had made the team but didn't want to seem overconfident.

We returned to the hotel, and they gathered us in a conference room. It was filled with anxiety because everyone knew that anyone who wanted to make the 1994 team had to be picked for the Finland trip. They started calling out names, and I quickly turned from confident to panic-stricken as names were called—but not mine. It still feels like a dream when I think about it. I was just frozen as they read out the last name, and it wasn't me.

I sat there stunned, and some guys looked at me and just shook their heads. I could not believe that I was not picked for that team. What had happened? It was the first time that I knew I'd been completely screwed. I was dumbfounded and was offered no explanation.

Some of the players who were picked had horrible camps but were either high draft picks or had been in the US system for years. I was an outsider and a newcomer, and I ended up getting the short end of the stick. It was a stunning and eye-opening experience.

It is not easy getting cut from a team that you thought you'd done everything to make. That taught me that life and sports are not fair sometimes. You are going to face adversity often in your life. No one is immune to this. Your response to this adversity is what matters. It is ultimately what decides your outcome as a player and as a person. This didn't change what I wanted my outcome to be as a player. It was just a setback.

I did eventually get picked for the USA Cup team in December, but it was of little consolation. Even though the rejection was tough, I made a name for myself in that camp. A number of agents approached me, and I did accept one's offer to go out to dinner. He had several stars in the NHL who had come out of college and thought I was on a similar track. I did eventually sign with him but not until after my senior year.

On to my junior year.

Junior Year

I had a lot riding on my junior year. I had to prove to the naysayers that I wasn't a one-hit wonder. I had to help get our program to the next level and build off what I'd accomplished in my sophomore year. I would be a prime target for our opponents, and I needed to find a way to fight through the adversity. As always, I came in great shape to camp. It was the one thing I could truly control.

The preseason was a very exciting time for me. Several publications picked me as a preseason All-American. Hockey East picked me as a first-team selection. There was a lot of pressure on me, and I was ready for the task. After a successful training camp, my season got off to a flying start.

We opened the season at Colgate University. They had a top-ranked team, and we were trying to establish ourselves as a top team in Hockey East. In that first game, I came out firing and ended up with two goals and an assist. I had several opportunities that I almost cashed in on, and, overall, I had a great game. Calgary scouts were at the game and had very positive things to say to me afterward. We quickly looked like we were a contending team in the league.

After that game, every team we faced focused on taking me away from the scoring sheet. It worked, and my scoring slowed down. But my assist production went way up, as I was finding different ways to impact the game. The only problem was that I needed to start scoring again.

Toward the end of the first half of the season, I was officially named to the Team USA roster for the USA Cup. It was a dream for me to be able to put on the USA jersey. It also seemed to help me get out of my goal-scoring slump. In the last weekend of the first half of the season, I recorded a hat trick and an assist against Northeastern University and scored a goal against an undefeated University of Maine team that had a rookie phenom, Paul Kariya, on its team. I was selected the Hockey East star of the week for that weekend.

Playing for Team USA in the USA Cup was a thrill and an eye-opening experience at the same time. For a kid whose single biggest inspiration was the Miracle on Ice, putting on that jersey was amazing. It didn't matter that I quickly realized that the majority, if not all, of the players on this team would not make the Olympic team. It extended my disappointment of not making that first team, but it was still a thrill.

Our first game was an exhibition against the Russian National team. We played them in Lake Placid, where the Miracle on Ice happened in 1980. We also dressed in the same room Team USA dressed that fateful night.

The Russians were a lot older and highly skilled. The game was played very differently on the Olympic-size ice sheet. It was the first game I played on a sheet of ice that big. It changes the way the game is played, and it took me a while to figure it out. We ended up tying the Russians, and I finished with one assist and a relatively solid game.

Next, we traveled down to Albany to play Team Canada. It was a back-and-forth game, and I played much better. I hit a crossbar and had an assist. We ended up losing by one goal, but it could have gone either way. It wasn't until recently that I discovered that I played against a future teammate and friend that night. John Spoltore scored for Canada. Several years later, I went on to play three seasons for the Louisiana IceGators with him.

It was a great experience, and I was excited to get back to the rest of our college schedule. We went on to have a great season, finishing third overall to the runaway champs UMaine and second-place Boston University. We knocked off Providence in the first round of the tournament and went on to face UMaine in the Hockey East Final 4.

UMaine was having one of the best seasons of any Division 1 team in history. They had lost only one game that season—an overtime loss to Boston University. Also, Paul Kariya was having one of the best seasons of any college hockey player ever and was only a freshman. Their team was loaded all over the place, with Jim Montgomery, the Ferraro twins, Patrice Tardif, etc. They were also backstopped by future Olympic teammates and NHL goalies Garth Snow and Mike Dunham. It was not an impossible task, but it was pretty close to it.

We gave UMaine a run for their money. The game went back and forth until the beginning of the third period. When the game was tied 4–4 and getting intense, I stole the puck just inside their blue line, fired a wrist shot, and scored in the top right corner to put us ahead 5–4. Maine was completely stunned and ended up pulling their goalie, Mike Dunham, who'd never been pulled from a game in his life.

Unfortunately, they brought Garth Snow in to settle them down, and they mounted a furious comeback. They ended up beating us 7–5 with an empty-net goal. We had a good chance to upset the eventual national champion, but we just couldn't hold them off any longer.

That game and the fact that New Hampshire lost to Boston University in their semifinal matchup set up a winner-take-all consolation game the next day. There were only twelve teams that made the NCAA tourney in 1993. Three would be chosen from each conference, and teams that had twenty or more wins would usually make it in. UMass Lowell and New Hampshire entered the game with nineteen wins each. Whoever won the consolation game would get the final Hockey East spot in the tourney.

The consolation game had a lot more riding on it than a normal consolation game ever did. It was a major opportunity for our university to take a giant step forward and get out from under the probation we were put on the year before. We needed this game, but so did New Hampshire.

It was the typical battle between our two teams that had played throughout the year. Each had beaten the other twice, and this would be the tie-breaker. We went back and forth and ended up tied at the end of regulation. In his speech before the overtime period, our coach kept emphasizing that we needed to win to get into the tourney.

It was a five-minute overtime. With under a minute left, one of our forwards rushed down the right side of the ice and threw the puck to the middle. I came flying in and one-timed it into the back of the net. The whole world went blank on me for a minute until I realized what I'd done. I looked up and saw our bench emptied and everyone racing toward me. The entire team mobbed me. Guys were screaming and practically in tears. I finished with two goals, including the overtime game-winner, in a 5–4 final.

The celebration continued on to the locker room. School officials and parents filled the room. The head coach came over to me with the biggest smile and hugged me. It was the biggest goal of my life on what was the biggest stage I had ever played on. The significance of the goal was enormous. It was only the second time in our school's history that we would make the NCAA tourney. More importantly, it lifted the cloud that our program had been under for the last few years.

We stayed for the final game between Maine and Boston University. Players were scattered throughout the Boston Garden, celebrating with our friends and family. After Maine won the championship, people looked for me to return to the ice surface. I was named to the Hockey East All-Tournament team for my efforts. I couldn't have been prouder to represent my team and university at that moment.

We made it back to campus that night and were looking forward to the NCAA selection show the following day. Our coach had to travel to Boston to take part in the selection show satellite. Meanwhile, our team and administration gathered at a local bar on Sunday night to see where we would be traveling to the following weekend.

Nearly three decades later, I can still vividly remember that night. As the selection show got underway, I could feel the energy in the room. Everyone was excited to move on from our past and take part in our first NCAA tourney under the new regime.

They started by naming the first three seeds in the East, which went pretty much as planned, then the top three seeds in the West. We figured we would probably be a fifth seed in the West or, at worst, a sixth seed in the East or West. Then they named seeds four through six in the East, and we weren't one of them.

Now it was the moment we had been waiting for.

They started naming the final seeds in the West and got to number five. Every seed up to that point had gone as planned. Then came the bombshell we didn't see coming. Brown University, with seventeen wins, was named the fifth seed. It was completely off the board. The sixth seed came and went, and I didn't even hear it.

We were left out of the tournament and totally screwed. You could hear a pin drop in that bar. Everyone was completely stunned. College careers ended that evening, and a giant opportunity was taken away from us. Later that night, the entire team got together and partied as a team one last time. It was a night to remember and to forget.

After that crushing night, I was able to reflect on the season a little bit. The Maine Black Bears went on to win the national championship and are now considered the best college hockey team of all time. Paul Kariya went on to score a hundred points and become the first freshman to win the Hobey Baker Award, which is given to the player considered the best in the country.

I was named to the Second Team All-Hockey East Team and the All-Tournament Team. I missed out on the All-American Team due to the arrival of Paul Kariya.

Probably my most cherished award came when Maine picked me as their Most Honored Opponent for that year. They had a team vote every year and flew the chosen player up for their banquet. Unfortunately, I missed the party because our team banquet happened to be on the same night. What a year!

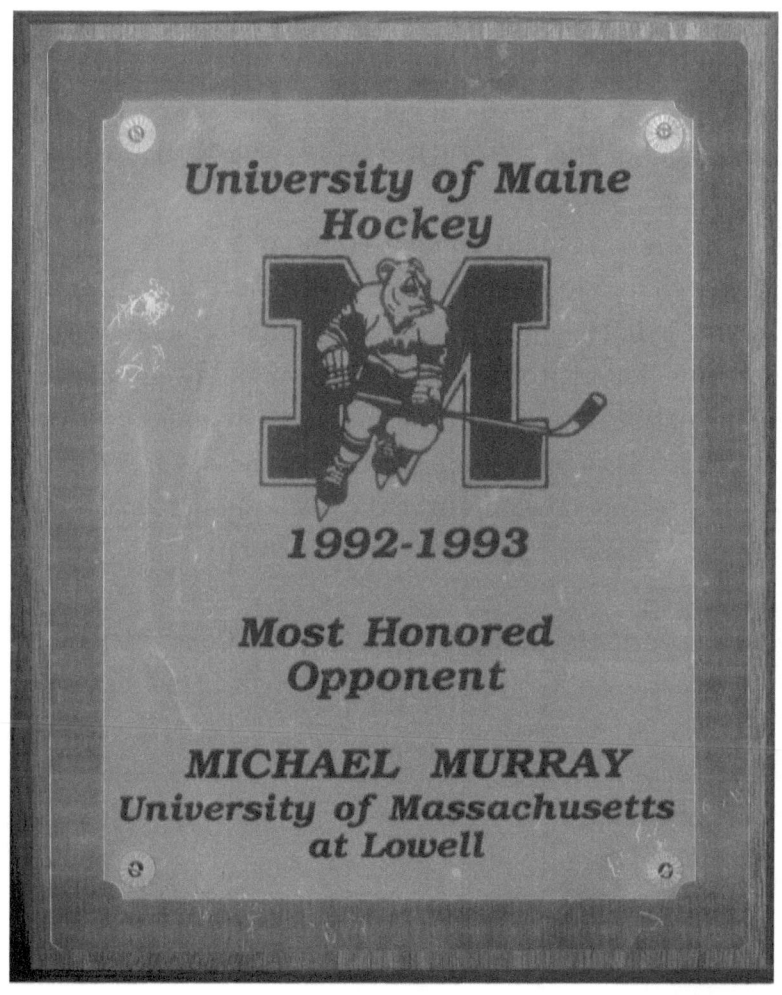

Senior Year

The summer going into my senior year ended up changing the course of my career. I had some interest from Calgary about forgoing my senior year and signing a professional contract with them. But I decided I wanted to stay and help my team win a national championship.

We had a very strong team returning. So, with some talented freshmen, we figured we could have a good run to the top. Also, on a personal note, I was going to be a leading candidate for the Hobey Baker Award and become an All-American.

Before I was fully committed to my senior year, I was invited to try out for the 1994 US Olympic team, which was playing in Lillehammer, Norway, in February. I knew it was a long shot, but with my strong junior year and strong showing in the national camp the previous year, I at least put myself in the discussion. It was no secret that this was my absolute dream, seeing as what effect the 1980 Miracle on Ice had on me. No doubt, looking back, this aspiration affected my judgment.

It was disappointing that the Olympic Committee threw the tryout together without a lot of thought. Apparently, the team was pretty much already picked. They gave most of the invitees only about a week or two to prepare for the tryout. Most of us had been off the ice for about a month and had just started our off-ice workout program.

I caught a bus in Boston with a bunch of other candidates from the Boston area and made the five-hour trek to Lake

Placid. To me, it was still a dream come true to make it this far from where I'd been only a few years earlier.

The first day of camp started with a regular practice followed by a scrimmage. Not only were the players not in skating shape, but the ice was also rough. My first practice went very well for me, and I was having a strong scrimmage, flying all around the ice and feeling pretty good.

With about a minute left in the scrimmage, I chased down a loose puck and went to take the body on an opposing player. As I was about to hit him, my foot got caught in a rut and stopped. But my body kept going. I felt an excruciating sharp pain that went through my right hip.

Well, little did I know, but this would be the beginning of the end of my mostly healthy career. I must have torn the labrum in my hip and subsequently tore cartilage in my right knee. The game ended quickly after my injury, and I struggled to get off the ice and into the dressing room. Getting back to the Olympic Village was a struggle. I had to walk very gingerly, and, unfortunately, my room was on the second floor. It was very painful to walk up and down the flight of stairs.

The next morning, I made it down to the trainer's room to get treatment. I could barely move but was determined to not miss a practice. The trainers were stunned that I was trying to play. I should have sought out some advice from my parents or agent. In Lake Placid, I felt pretty isolated from the rest of the world. Back then, we did not have cell phones for a quick call or text for advice like we do now. Looking back, talking to my parents or agent probably would have helped in deciding whether to play through the injury or not.

It had taken me a long time to get to this moment, and I was absolutely not going to sit out. Day after day, I did as much rehab as possible and made it to each practice or scrimmage. Even though I was a long shot, it was frustrating that I couldn't play up to my ability.

Looking back, I'm not sure I would have done things much differently. Playing in the Olympics was truly one of my dreams, and putting my college and pro career at risk seemed worth it.

I will say that if I knew how much this injury would affect the rest of my career, I might have had second thoughts. I do wish the decision had been taken out of my hands. Somebody should have forced me not to play. But I was a grown man at the time and could have made that call. I just couldn't have lived with myself if I hadn't given it everything I had. *No regrets.*

The camp ended with a thud. We all left with the coaching staff saying they would get back to us with their decision. On the bus ride back, we all talked about how disappointing the tryout was. I was surprised at how rinky-dink the operation was. It was unorganized, and I realized that most of the team had been picked before we even got there.

It still amazes me that the Olympic team's general manager was a former high school hockey coach from Minnesota. It truly was the old boys' network, and I was an outsider. It is funny that the coach of the 1984 team never played hockey. This is probably why the team didn't have a lot of success after the 1980 games.

On to my senior year.

Putting the disappointment of the Olympic tryout behind me, I focused on preparing for my senior season and put together a rigorous training regimen for the rest of the summer. I wanted to break all my previous records in the gym and be in absolutely the best shape of my life.

I set some personal goals for myself and was determined to accomplish all of them. Chief among them was earning the Hobey Baker Award, achieving All-American status, and being the top scorer in the nation. After my junior season, these goals were well within my reach. To back up these goals, I was picked as a preseason Hockey East All-Star and preseason All-American. *The Hockey News* picked me as one of the top ten candidates and only one of four forwards for the Hobey Baker Award. I was on a mission to accomplish all of these goals and win a national championship.

FEATURE

Big man on campus
Who will replace Maine's Kariya as college hockey's best player?

By Kevin Allen

November could be considered audition month in U.S. college hockey. It's a time when several stars are competing for the role as leading man in 1993-94.

Maine Black Bears' left winger Paul Kariya, last year's Hobey Baker Award winner, has the job until early December, at which point he'll join the Canadian Olympic team.

Who will take over after that is unclear. Here's a list of 10 understudies who should challenge for center stage in the National Collegiate Athletic Association. Players are listed alphabetically, along with the league in which they play–Central Collegiate Hockey Association, Eastern College Athletic Conference, Hockey East or Western Collegiate Hockey Association.

Jim Carey, G, Wisconsin (WCHA). Two years ago the Badger coaching staff couldn't get Carey an invitation to USA Hockey's Select-17 camp. Today, he might be the most talented goaltender in college hockey. As an 18-year-old freshman, he had a 3.07 goals-against average and a 26-15-1 record.

Brian Holzinger, C, Bowling Green (CCHA). Many coaches feel U.S. Olympic team coach Tim Taylor erred in cutting Holzinger. Now they'll have to deal with the gifted center, who scored 31 goals in 41 games last season and was named a second-team CCHA all-star in his sophomore year.

Kaj Linna, D, Boston University (HE). Enjoy him while you can, because he won't be coming back for his senior season. League rivals can't believe an NHL organization didn't draft the 6-foot-2, 192-pound Finnish blueliner after his sophomore year.

"There's no question he'll be among the top defensemen in the country," said Terriers' coach Jack Parker.

Neil Little, G, Rensselaer Polytechnic Institute (ECAC). At 6-foot-1, 185 pounds, Little isn't exactly a Redwood. But he's filling a lot more of the net than he did last year, when he went 19-9-3 with a .906 save percentage and 2.93 goals-against aver-

power forward goes to the net well and has a decent touch. Murray had 23 goals and 81 points in 39 games last season.

"Some guys have harder shots, but when he shoots, the puck goes by the goaltender," Parker said.

Jamie Ram, G, Michigan Tech (WCHA). Ram was the nation's busiest goalie in 1992-93, playing 36 games. His talent is the main reason why the Huskies have a chance to make their first NCAA tournament appearance since 1981.

leading the Tigers to their first sweep of the Minnesota Golden Gophers since 1980-81.

Steve Shields, G, Michigan (CCHA). It's amazing Shields doesn't receive more recognition. He has won 83 games over the past three seasons and his goals-against average has dropped each year. He led the CCHA with a 2.22 GAA last year.

Sean Tallaire, RW, Lake Superior State (CCHA). Lakers' coach Jeff Jackson is a booster of senior Clayton Beddoes because he is

Mass.-Lowell center Mike Murray may not be the most talented player in the NCAA, but the power forward knows how to score.

"He gives us confidence," coach Bob Mancini said. "When he's playing, our shoulders are higher and our

among college hockey's most consistent scorers. But rivals are more fearful of sophomore Tallaire. He

There was only one problem with my plan: the nagging pain in my knee and hip. The nightmare of my senior year was just beginning. I had given my hip sufficient time off after the injury and was able to attack my training regimen for most of the summer. But a few days before school started, I began having increasing pain in the side of my knee. When I got on campus, I immediately went to the training staff and got it checked out.

Seeing that I'd had the hip injury in May and now was having knee pain, they thought the knee pain was related to the hip. The staff diagnosed it as IT band syndrome and recommended rest. They did not want me to do any activity on my legs and hoped the inflammation would resolve itself.

A few days into school, the team got together and did physical testing. I had the record for bench press and squat from the previous year. I was able to best those records by benching 340 pounds and squatting nearly 500 pounds. I was in the best shape of my life despite the knee pain but was ordered to rest.

There was no question that my success had a lot to do with the physical shape I was in. I was ready to have the best year of my life, but I continued to have the nagging pain despite the rest. The medical staff assured me over and over that the pain had nothing to do with my knee because it was tendinitis from my IT band.

If you know anything about hockey, you know that your legs are the key to everything. The advice I received was to do nothing with my legs and let them rest, which ended up being not the best advice. This delayed my diagnosis, and my problems snowballed from there.

The month before the season started in October was the most frustrating and helpless month of my life. It was also the most important time of my career. I had built my success on the strength I received from training. I know I worked harder than most, and it ended up being the edge that brought me success. This was taken away from me and set the course for the worst hockey year of my life.

The NCAA allowed the team to touch the ice for the first time on October 1. The medical staff decided to let me join my teammates that day. About halfway through practice, I could feel my knee stiffening up. By the end of practice, I could barely push off on my leg. I knew something was drastically wrong.

After I got off the ice, the medical staff checked me out and decided to get me an MRI. Amazingly, they were still assuring me that it was my hip and that there was a one-in-a-million chance that it was anything with my knee. When the results came back, wouldn't you know it? I had a significant tear in the cartilage of my right knee.

They told me, "You know that one in a million? Well, you're the one."

I said, "You have got to be kidding me."

I was completely screwed.

Within a few days, I was in a surgery room getting operated on. It wasn't bad enough that I had surgery, but I had done nothing to prepare myself to recover from it. I hadn't done anything on my legs in four weeks. Great advice. After the surgery, I had a week off before I hit the ice again. The rehab

I did was a complete joke. I should have gone to a physical therapist, but our athletic trainer oversaw my recovery. Big mistake. In his defense, he did not know how to rehab a hurt knee.

By the time I hit the ice and jumped into a Division 1 practice, I had been off my legs for six weeks. I was physically unprepared to play at that level. My calling card was being in better shape than everyone else, and now it was the opposite.

I missed the first weekend of the year, as the team was out at the Air Force Academy to open up the season. I was the captain, and I missed the road trip. This couldn't have been a worse start to my year.

The team got off to a great start, and the emergence of a star freshman took the league by storm. Greg Bullock opened up the season with three goals in the first two games. By the time I got back into the lineup the following weekend, the pressure couldn't have been any higher for me. I was behind the eight ball.

I was trying to work myself back into shape because of the poor advice and rehab I'd received. Things seemed to go downhill quickly. I'd been a mainstay of the power play for the last two years, and now I was losing playing time. So I pressed more and more, trying to reestablish my presence. Nothing seemed to work. But I continued to work harder and harder until I finally started to turn the corner.

In a game the week before Thanksgiving, I was cross-checked in my right hip and got a severe hip pointer. I was a target for every team we played against, and since I was returning from knee surgery, cheap shots were happening on a regular basis. It came with the territory, but I didn't have to like it. This hip pointer was one of the painful injuries I had to deal with in my career. Everything from sneezing to coughing to going to the bathroom was excruciating.

I missed another team trip, this time to Vermont over Thanksgiving weekend. The year couldn't have gotten off to a worse start. And there wasn't anything I could do to stop it. Anything that could go wrong did go wrong. Not only that, but I also couldn't believe how quickly the coaching staff seemed to have abandoned me.

My senior year never got back on track, and I could sense it fading away. So much promise and so many dreams were slipping away. But one thing saved my life that year. Meeting my future wife was the greatest thing that happened to me, and she kept me sane as I was struggling through the year.

Joy and I were set up on a blind date a week before I was operated on. We instantly connected and were inseparable from there on out. In fact, we had so much in common that we seemed to have known each other from a past life. Joy was the prettiest and most genuine person I'd ever met. She was the school's star tennis player, and pretty much everyone wanted to date her. I can honestly say I don't know what I would have done without her.

Thankfully, with Joy by my side, I was able to focus on staying positive and making the most of the rest of the year. We had a great team, and I wanted to make sure I was healthy and playing my best at the end of the year. So I continued to rehab and work as hard as I could to finish with a bang. Even though I was having a tough year, Calgary was still very positive about my future. I had no choice but to put my dreams aside and finish strong.

Our team had a great regular season and finished with only eight losses—our best season since UMass Lowell entered Division 1 play ten years earlier. We made it to the Hockey East Finals and lost to Boston University by a score of 4–3.

We met as a team the next night and watched the NCAA selection show. The experience was similar to the year before, when they started announcing the seeds in the East. We figured we would be the third seed in the East based on our second-place finish in Hockey East. When they announced the seedings and we were not in the top three, it was like déjà vu. We could hear everyone's hearts drop when they started announcing the West seeds. We couldn't believe this was happening again.

They got to the third seed in the West and, to our relief, announced UMass Lowell as the team. The crowd erupted in applause. We would be facing the number-six seed, with the first two seeds getting a bye. Michigan State hosted the West regionals at their arena, and, to our shock, the number-six seed ended up being Michigan State. What a sham. We were playing the lowest seed in their home rink in front of their fans. It was just one more obstacle we had to overcome.

We played in front of a packed house, with the majority of the fans cheering for Michigan State. Michigan was also in the regional, and their band actually played for us. We got out to an early lead and held on for a 4–3 win. I had the eventual game-winning goal late in the second period. When I broke into the middle of Michigan State's zone, a teammate fed me a pass, and I beat the goalie high over the glove.

It was one of my best all-around games of the year. Along with the goal, I hit a crossbar on a partial breakaway. Defensively, I also saved a goal at the crease late in the game. Michigan State's star player, Anson Carter, had a wide-open net with a few minutes to play. Out of desperation, I hooked his stick at the last second and stole the puck from him. Michigan State had all the momentum, and if they'd scored at that time, we would have been in real trouble.

After the game, I talked with the Calgary scouts. They came away very impressed with my overall game—particularly my defensive play—and projected me as a two-way power forward. No doubt, this helped me get signed to an NHL contract later that summer.

The very next night, we faced Minnesota, which had a bye the night before. The winner would go to the Frozen Four—the Division 1 semifinals and championship games. We dominated most of the game and held a 1–0 lead late into the game. We did have several chances to increase the lead but failed to capitalize.

In the second period, I broke down the right wing and blasted a slap shot that hit the post. It went on the ice far side and beat the goalie, but it ended up rolling on its side and just missing the goal.

Late in the third period, Minnesota wrapped a puck around our net. Their left wing picked it off the boards and fired it at the net. It surprised our goalie and beat him short side. The game went to two overtimes, and we ended up losing on a partial breakaway goal. Unfortunately, we were exhausted from playing the night before. Minnesota was well rested and had a clear advantage, especially with the game going to two overtimes. My nightmare of a season finally came to an end. But I did end up turning my season around and finished strong enough to sign a three-year NHL contract.

As disappointing as the year had been on a personal level, I have no regrets over how I handled it. I went into camp in the best shape of my life, broke all my lifting records, and was prepared to have my greatest season. Maybe it would have been different if I hadn't been ready for the season, but that was not the case. It was certainly very frustrating, but *no regrets.*

I was more or less a walk-on when I arrived at UML and had turned myself into one of the top players in college hockey by the time I left. Going from a fourth liner as a freshman to signing an NHL contract in four years was more than I could have ever dreamed of. Leaving UML as the second-leading goal scorer in school history despite the challenging senior year is something that I am very proud of.

Chapter 6
Flames

"What matters is not the size of the dog in the fight, but
the size of the fight in the dog."

—Bear Bryant

A fter the season ended, I officially picked Lewis Gross as
my agent. He had pursued me since my sophomore year
and had most of the top college players in the East as clients.
It seemed like a pretty easy decision. We started negotiating
right away and were in talks to sign and join the Calgary
Flames minor league AHL team in Saint John, New Brunswick,
before the end of the school year.

The first contract I signed happened to be a hockey card
contract with Classic Cards. They paid me $5,000 and built
in incentives if I played in the NHL as a rookie. It was nice to
finish my college year with a little money in my pocket.

It took most of the summer to finally reach an agreement
with the Calgary Flames. They signed me to an entry-level

three-year contract. They paid me a $100,000 bonus and would pay me $60,000 in the minors and *$250,000 if I played in the NHL.*

This was a dream come true. My goalie at UMass Lowell, Dwayne Roloson, also signed a three-year contract with the Flames. We went on to play seven years of hockey together. He was also responsible for setting me up on a blind date with Joy. I guess I kind of owe him for that.

I spent the summer training and getting ready for my first pro camp and season. I even put in some time boxing with my high school football coach. Unfortunately, I was still having some trouble with my right knee and went to see a physical therapist. They discovered that I had some significant weakness in my right leg and were surprised at the lack of therapy I received at UMass Lowell. This put me at a disadvantage when I entered my first camp.

Rookie camp started in Calgary a few weeks before the big camp opened. It got our feet wet heading into NHL camp. We were also training with the Japanese National Team. They were very talented but weak. The culture was also unfamiliar to us. Younger players didn't want to beat older players out of respect. This isn't exactly the best attitude to have when you're trying to compete at a high level.

The Calgary coach, Dave King, had spent a number of years teaching the game over in Japan, and he'd invited them to train with us. At the end of the week, we scrimmaged. We were all chomping at the bit to impress the coaching staff. But, in some respects, we did the opposite.

We ended up running over Japan and dominated them. I had a few goals and a few big hits. At the end of the first period, Dave King came down and read us the riot act. He was pissed that we were killing them physically. He ordered us to stop hitting them because we were embarrassing them. What a strange message to send to a bunch of rookies trying to impress the NHL staff. No wonder Calgary had been struggling since winning the Stanley Cup in 1989.

The NHL camp started a few weeks after we arrived in Calgary. The amount of talent and number of fights made for an *eye-opening* experience. Fighting was banned in college hockey but there was no question that players who grew up playing in Canada had a clear advantage in the on-the-ice fighting.

They'd grown up fighting, as it was part of their culture. My boxing experience made me more than capable of fighting off the ice. But fighting on the ice was a completely different experience. It was more about grappling and balancing. There is no question that we Americans needed to learn how to fight. Otherwise, it could end very badly for us. Seeing that I played a very physical game, fighting was inevitable. I did end up having a few scraps in camp, but nothing major.

Toward the end of camp, we played in the annual Red vs White game in a small rink near the Saddledome. I was in the starting lineup in front of a sold-out crowd of roughly three thousand fans. It was humorous when, as they announced the starting lineup, players like Phil Housley, Gary Roberts, and Steve Chiasson got standing ovations. When they announced me, the crowd fell mostly silent. No doubt they were trying to figure out who I was.

I had a very solid game, laying out several big hits and collecting a few assists. It looked like I made enough of an impression to get myself in an exhibition game and earn an opportunity to make the big club. That never happened, as I saw a number of first-round picks who didn't deserve an opportunity get one. It was my first, but not my last, experience watching high draft picks get their shot even though they didn't deserve it.

A few weeks into camp, I was called into the office and sent down to the team's AHL affiliate in Saint John, New Brunswick. They felt I'd had a strong camp but said I needed work in the minors. However, there wasn't much room in Calgary's lineup.

After I reported to camp in Saint John, the NHL decided to lock out their players. The season was delayed due to the lockout of players imposed by the NHL franchises. The lockout was a subject of dispute as the players sought collective bargaining and owners sought to help teams in weaker markets as well as make sure they could cap the rising salaries of players. After a new labor agreement was reached between the owners and the NHL Players' Association, the season finally began but would be reduced to forty-eight games rather than the standard eighty-two, making it the shortest season in fifty-three years. The season started on January 20, 1995. That didn't help me or other rookies because Calgary sent a number of players from the big club to play in the minors until the lockout ended. That meant I didn't get the opportunity to play as much as I needed. It stunted my development a little until the lockout ended in January.

Saint John was quite a shock for me after I'd spent a month in beautiful Calgary. Saint John is a small seaport city northeast of Maine. It was economically depressed, but, like most Canadian cities, it was hockey crazy. It seemed that the biggest line of work in the area was driving a taxi. They had the equivalent of one taxicab driver for every four citizens. That greatly benefitted those of us who didn't have transportation to get around the city.

Living in a new country and new city presented a lot to get used to. The city was very different from what I was used to, from the Canadian dollar to TV to newspapers to the food. I didn't like any of it. The people were the only saving grace.

They were rabid hockey fans but also, in my experience, great people.

We quickly prepared and entered the exhibition season when we traveled to northern Quebec to face the Montreal Canadiens farm team in a small town hours away from Saint John. Pulling into this town in the middle of nowhere was eye-opening. They had one motel and, apparently, no restaurants. We checked into the motel, which seemed to be out of some low-budget horror film. We gathered for our pregame meal in the motel lobby and forced down a horrible meal.

The game-day routine was also drastically different from what I was used to in college. We had a pregame skate at ten a.m. Then we had a team pregame meal at one p.m. for a seven p.m. game. After the one p.m. meal, everyone settled down for a pregame nap until waking around four p.m. This later became one of my favorite parts of being a professional athlete—guilt-free naps! After waking, I would grab a small snack, usually a Snickers bar or toast. Then I'd be at the rink by five p.m.

In college, the routine was much different. We usually had no pregame skate because we were in class during the day. After class, we had our meal around three p.m. for a seven p.m. game. There was no pregame nap, and we never had a snack before the game. I always still showed up for the game about two hours before game time.

As I prepared for the Fredericton Canadiens game, I understood that I would need, at some point, to get into a fight. It was a necessary part of the game, even for players who weren't so-called tough guys. It was drastically different from how we prepared in college. Now we knew we could be in a bare-knuckle fight at any moment.

Most of the tough guys I played with in my pro career did not scare me when we were off the ice. I did not hesitate to throw down if necessary. On the ice, though, it was different. You needed to know where to grab an opponent's arms. A majority of fights were no more than a grappling wrestling match. The secret was to get the opponent off balance and control their throwing arm. When that was achieved, you could inflict great damage to your opponent's face.

The French Canadians were very different from the English-speaking Canadians. They have wanted to secede from the rest of Canada for generations and were not shy about expressing that desire. My French-Canadian teammates usually stuck together and were more European in nature than other Canadians. It was very interesting to watch the dynamics between the French Canadians and the rest of the team. It was as if they thought they had invented the game and no one else could ever understand or play it as well as they could.

I grew up hating the Montreal Canadiens, much like I hated the Yankees. But my feelings for the two teams were a little different. The Montreal fans' arrogance irritated me as a Bruins fan more than the Yankee fans' attitude did. I went on to play the Canadiens a dozen times that year and got into my first two pro fights against them.

I was unquestionably anxious before the game that resulted in my first fight, and I was looking for a fight. I knew my style of play would involve a few scraps. I needed that physical style if I wanted to make it to the ultimate level. I was committed to playing my power forward role—one that blended physical and offensive skills.

As I went out for warm-ups, it became obvious that we were in hostile territory. It seemed the whole town had come out for the game and were wearing their Montreal Canadiens jerseys. It was one of the loudest arenas I had ever played in. It fit a few thousand fans, and they were there for their one chance to watch and cheer for the future of their beloved team.

As the game started, I could feel that it was not going to be a normal hockey game. Everyone on the ice wanted to prove that they belonged in the NHL. These games were typically a fight fest. And when they ended, we didn't remember if we won or lost the game. We just remembered how we did in the fights. And since this particular game was in the middle of Montreal Canadiens territory, that hostile competition only intensified. There were plenty of tough guys on both sides of the ice, and they didn't disappoint.

Toward the end of the first period, I raced to the front of the Canadiens net on a typical three-on-two. As the puck deflected into the corner, the defenseman on the Canadiens slashed me in the back of the leg. Without hesitation, I turned around and engaged the player. As I was getting my bearings, I took a few shots to the head that did not seem to do much. I then proceeded to start throwing punches at my opponent.

After the first few shots, I landed a haymaker. My fist connected perfectly with his nose, and I knocked him clear off his feet. It was right out of a movie. His nose exploded, and I landed on top of him in what was a decisive victory.

The referee escorted me to the penalty box. But wow! My first fight could not have gone any better. I was still jacked up about the fight and sat there in amazement. As I looked across the ice at my bench, I was stunned at what I saw. The whole bench was hysterically laughing—players, coaches, and trainers. I couldn't figure out what was going on. I thought they would be incredibly impressed by what they'd just witnessed, but they weren't.

The delay in the game seemed to go on for a few minutes. The referees were talking with some fans in the crowd in what seemed to be a prolonged negotiation. Eventually, the referee came over and handed my hockey gloves to me. I was curious as to why my gloves had been in the stands. The referee was laughing along with most people at the rink.

In hockey fights, it is customary to throw your gloves down to the ice as you start throwing punches. Apparently, I'd done just the opposite. I was so excited to fight that I accidently threw my gloves up into the stands. I guess no one had ever done that before. Our team had to offer a few items to the fans in exchange for my gloves. Oh well. At least I won the fight.

The professional hockey lifestyle in the top minor league was an unbelievable experience. The AHL was the top league for NHL prospects to play in. Every game was intense. Rosters were filled with first-round picks, former NHL players, and excellent players who may have had one deficiency in their game that kept them out of the NHL.

The Maritime Division that I played in was considered maybe the worst division in pro sports—not because of the competition but because of the location. Although we made the occasional trip to the US, we spent the majority of our time in Saint John, Fredericton, Prince Edward Island, Cape Breton, and St John's in Canada.

The weather was the real problem, along with a depressed economy and extremely high tax rate. We chartered flights to most of our games, and our home arena was first class. I hear that the area is beautiful in the summer. Unfortunately, the time I spent there was more than gloomy.

The people made up for it, as they were incredible and treated us like royalty. Many dinners were comped, and we never had to pay for many drinks at the bars. When it came to nightlife, we were always escorted through lines and never paid any cover charges. It's funny because when we made trips to the United States, players expected the same treatment. I had to laugh because I knew it wouldn't happen. And it didn't.

My first year in the pros was very similar to my first year in college. As the year went on, I started to figure out the game. I was constantly improving, and, with my extra ice time after the lockout ended, my game started to take off. There were plenty of games in which I was dominant and played more consistently.

The problem was that at the pro level, we had to be consistent every game. We were entitled to nothing. I needed to figure out that piece to make the leap to the next level.

One day, I was walking around a bookstore and stumbled on a book written by James E. Loehr titled *Mental Toughness Training for Sports.* The book hit home for me and let me look at the actual game in a different way. It almost immediately paid dividends.

I've probably read the book close to ten times over the years. It just triggered me in a positive way. There's one passage in the book that I read weekly during the rest of the season to remind me of the importance of moment-to-moment focus.

I have learned to focus on the MOMENT. I savor the moment. Every moment of every performance is something to be fully experienced and enjoyed. I take each moment for what it is, and whenever I do that, I immediately experience a sense of calm, strength, and energy. I seem to glow inside.

When I savor the moment, a new and powerful source of energy gets released within me. I immediately feel more positive and more in control. Things start flowing automatically. There's no tension, no anxiety, no fear. As soon as I lose this moment, however, as soon as I start thinking about winning and losing, what I should have done or what could happen, all the negatives come charging back.

. . . I perform best when I savor the moment, when I am right here and now and love every minute of it. As long as what I'm physically doing at the moment is what I am mentally doing at the moment, everything happens naturally. I don't have to get psyched or try to concentrate or try to perform well. I just do it. And when I'm there, I've got excess energy, and I'm mentally on target. My mind and body seem to click . . .

The price that I paid to reach this point has been high. I wonder if it was all that necessary. As I reflect back on the years of struggle . . . Why was it so hard? What made the whole thing so damned difficult?

The answer is painfully clear—I did! I kept getting in the way. I was bound and determined to succeed, and I wanted to win at all costs . . . I wanted to prove to myself and to everyone else that I could do it. My answer was simple: try harder and be stronger. No one ever told me that trying softer, not harder, might be the key, or that inner calmness would bring strength. The anger, frustration, agony, and disappointment were not so much from losing as from knowing that I performed considerably below what I was capable of doing. When I wanted it most, I was incapable of performing well. And the reason is now clear–I tried TOO hard: I was forcing it.

For me, trying to play better, trying not to get angry, trying to concentrate, or trying not to be nervous made the situation worse. I was fighting the current rather than going with it.

I used to worry about the guy on the other side. I understand now that it's me, not him, that I should be concerned with . . . I've always been my own toughest opponent, and I suppose I always will be. Savoring the moment . . . does two things: it brings me back to doing what I'm doing and it suddenly makes it fun again. Playing my best always seems to happen when I am feeling a particular way. I feel pumped-up, positive, confident, and invincible. . . . When I stay with the moment, the feelings are much easier to keep, and when I lose them, I can get them back in the same way.

Don't misunderstand. The feelings don't always come . . . I'm still my own toughest opponent, but I'm winning that contest most of the time now. . . . The right feelings come when I live in every moment, when I love and savor every moment—when I am in the NOW!

Reading this book and that passage helped get me to the next level of my development. The sign of a great athlete is consistently performing at a high level. I would read that passage often throughout the rest of my career as a reminder to stay in the moment. I was never going to be the most talented player, but I could control my consistency in play.

Coaches were looking for reliable players they could count on. As my play became more consistent, my ice time started to reflect that. My confidence grew, and I started to produce. I was the most improved player on the team by the end of the season.

We made the playoffs but unfortunately made a quick exit. I learned a lot during the season and made adjustments as the year went on. I felt very confident at the end of the year that I would make a similar jump in my second year like I did in college.

Second Year

That summer, I had a renewed commitment to training. I learned so much in my first year and now knew what I needed to do to prepare for the upcoming season. Every summer, I incorporated different training techniques into my routines: running hills at Diamond Hill near where I grew up, cardio training, working on the mental side of the game, and doing anything to get an edge. It was also my first injury-free summer in a couple of years. I was determined to put myself in the best position to make it to the NHL that year.

Training camp was moved to Saint John in my second year because the Calgary Saddledome was undergoing renovations. I went into camp in great shape and got off to a quick start. I was scoring in intrasquad games and opening a lot of eyes with my play. Many in the front office were pulling me aside and telling me how good I was playing.

Unfortunately, I was sent down to the minors toward the end of camp. I was told that I made great strides and that they were very happy with my development. But they wanted to get me more playing time in the minors, where I would get prime minutes in all areas of the game.

I built tremendous confidence in my game through the training camp and carried that into the minor league season. I was playing more minutes than any other forward and playing in all the critical times of the game (i.e., power play, penalty kill, and end of games). My game was coming along, and I was being rewarded in the process.

We had a very demanding first-year coach, and, as good as I was playing, the atmosphere was absolutely miserable. Players were on edge even on off days. He was an old-school coach who was trying to build ten years of mental toughness into the first few months of the season.

He was playing constant mind games with the entire team. On a few occasions, we got together as a team and discussed going on strike and not showing up for a practice. Since the team was very young, we decided against it. Nobody wanted to put their careers in jeopardy.

Despite the miserable atmosphere he created, I did learn a lot. One line that stuck with me was "If winning was easy, then everyone would do it." I modified that quote years later for the teams I ended up coaching.

The coach selected me as one of the team captains, which was a big honor in my second season as a pro. I took the selection very seriously.

My production as a two-way forward was improving. Not only was I contributing offensively, but I was also playing great defense and being a physical presence. I also learned some things the hard way. The process of becoming a great pro was not always easy.

We played one game in Syracuse, New York, against the Syracuse Crunch. I was coming off probably my best game as a pro hockey player. I was filled with confidence and maybe took the process for granted.

That quickly changed when I got off to a slow start in the first period. I didn't think I was playing poorly, but I wasn't up to the standard I had set for myself. Before I knew it, I was benched in the second period. It definitely caught me by surprise and drove home the message that I was not entitled to anything. I was not a first-round pick. I wasn't overly talented and certainly had not proven myself as a pro long enough to be given the benefit of the doubt. Lesson learned.

Even with that little blip, I was getting a lot of praise from the coaching staff, and word was trickling down from Calgary that they were also very happy. A few of our players who'd started off in Calgary and were sent down were filling me in.

At that time, Calgary did not call up players too frequently. That was mostly because its NHL team location was over four hours away by plane, and the team management was cheap. I knew if I kept improving and bided my time, I would be recalled at some point.

One day before a November practice, the coach called a meeting. As always, the team tensed up as he walked into the room. I started to read the coach like a poker player. He would glare at players and make them look away to intimidate them. I started to figure this out and had a response that would help me then and in life after hockey.

As the coach walked in the room, I would not look away. If he looked my way, I would just look back at him. I wouldn't glare. I would just continue to look at him until he looked away. The first one to look away loses. It worked every time he tried to stare me down. I went on to use this trick as an adult—particularly in interview situations.

As the coach walked in the room that November day, he handed out pens and pieces of paper to everyone. We were all pretty confused about what was going on. He went on to ask us to write down who we thought was the team MVP—the most reliable player up to that point in the season.

I can't even remember who I wrote down. Once the coach collected all the papers, he called out the names people had written down. At the end of the count, I received about 75 percent of the vote. He then pulled out a paper and started to read it.

"The Calgary Flames," he said, "have recalled from the Saint John Flames . . ."

Holy shit! I thought. *I'm getting called up.*

But the name announced was not mine.

Most of the team just looked at me and then quickly cheered for the teammate whose name was just called. He was a former first-round pick who had not lived up to expectations. When the coach had taken over that year, he decided to turn him into his project and revive his career. He was playing well but was nothing but a third-line player at that point.

There was no doubt that I was a little stunned. For a moment, I'd thought my lifelong dream had come true. I had to collect myself right away, be a good teammate, and offer my congratulations. Many players came over to me privately and told me how ridiculous the coach's announcement had been. I'm not sure why Coach decided to do that in that manner. Regardless, it backfired on him because he was wrong about how he thought the vote would go.

I had to put my disappointment aside and move on. This was just another step in my journey to the NHL. I was on too much of a roll to let this bother me. It was crazy that the coach had done that, though.

Fast-forward a few weeks, and my life would change forever.

Chapter 7
The Day After

"It's not whether you get knocked down,
it's whether you get up."
—Vince Lombardi

December 29, 1995, changed the trajectory of my life. It was also the day after the worst and best day of my life. I was still processing what happened the day before, getting into two fights then receiving great news about getting called up to the NHL for the first time. I had to get focused and ready for our game against the Prince Edward Island Senators. I definitely had confidence in my walk that day. To hear the coach tell me I would be getting called up and that it was only a matter of time filled me with incredible motivation.

Nothing other than his statement really sticks out in my memory. Players were still buzzing about the fights, but now the focus turned to the night's game. Just like in the last handful of games, the coach started me regardless of which line was starting. I was the team's biggest hitter, and he wanted to set the tone for the game.

I was determined to get the game going and lay a big hit to start the game. I skated around the ice in warm-ups and felt incredible. I felt fast and incredibly pumped.

The referee dropped the puck, and play started. The puck was dumped into our zone, and we then broke the puck out. The puck went to our left winger. He got over the red line and dumped the puck into the far corner. The opposing defensemen collected the puck and passed it up to the winger on my boards.

I was flying in at top speed and went to level a big hit. As I went to deliver the hit, their winger tried to avoid me. As I went to lunge at him, our shoulders glanced off each other. But our knees hit straight on.

Then boom.

I felt a snap and crumbled to the ice. As I attempted to get up, I knew something was terribly wrong. I called over to the bench for help. It was about eighteen seconds into the game, and my night was over.

The doctors did a quick evaluation and decided I needed to go to the hospital for X-rays. Their feeling was that maybe I'd dislocated the kneecap, but they wanted to make sure. They just told me to bring the X-rays back to the rink. I was loaded into an ambulance and went to the local hospital.

When I arrived at the hospital—still in most of my hockey gear—they wheeled me into the X-ray room and took the X-ray. I sat in a room by myself and, after a number of minutes, flagged down a nurse. I told her I needed a copy of the X-rays to take back to the arena. She responded very quickly and told me I wasn't going anywhere.

She said that my right leg was broken.

I sat there in stunned silence for what seemed like an eternity until I spoke up and told someone that I needed a phone. One of the nurses wheeled me into a private room so I could call Joy, my girlfriend.

That was a tough call. As soon as I heard her voice, I broke down and cried. When I called her, she realized I was supposed to be playing a hockey game and that this couldn't be good news. I was devastated and in disbelief that this could happen. It was just a very bad dream I could not wake from.

Unfortunately, it was only a few days after Christmas, and our head orthopedic doctor was on vacation. I didn't really know the backup doctor. But he explained that he would be doing surgery to stabilize the knee. It seemed to be pretty straightforward. I had been through this once before, so I knew the drill.

They transferred me to another hospital for the surgery. Afterward, I spent the next week or so stuck in a hospital in Saint John. Unfortunately, I had been in the hospital several times in the United States, and I recognized the difference in care. For example, my bed was manually operated. That meant that any time I needed to raise or lower the bed, I needed to call a nurse and have them do it. More often than not, it took forty-five minutes to an hour for a nurse to get to my room because the hospital was so understaffed. They would spend a few minutes adjusting the bed and then leave. Of course, once they left, I would be uncomfortable again. I felt bad calling them again and would hold off as long as I could until I had to call again.

Needless to say, even though US healthcare is expensive and has its own problems, I would take it every day of the week. The people in Canada were nice, but the care and facilities were a couple of decades behind.

The Calgary Flames agreed to fly me back home for a few weeks. When I got there, my parents insisted that I see an orthopedic doctor in Providence. Dr. Fadele was the head team doctor for the Providence Bruins and an acquaintance of a family friend. I had already been through a broken leg in high school, and the doctor in Saint John told me I would be back playing in three to four months. So I wasn't worried about the appointment.

That quickly changed when I met with the doctor. Within minutes, he got very honest about my situation. He told me it was a really bad break and that I had broken my knee joint's articular cartilage. He explained that the shiny coating of a chicken bone is the articular cartilage. Unfortunately, once you damage that cartilage, it cannot grow back.

He broke the news that this could be a career-ending injury. I just sat there in shock. He also told me that he would have done a different surgery and placed two screws in the bone to secure it better. He would also put me in a hinged cast so I could get blood flow to the area.

The doctor in Saint John inserted one screw and put me in a hip-to-ankle cast for four to six weeks. It was a very delicate injury that required blood flow for healing. But it was too late to go in and do surgery to secure the joint, so I had to wait until the bone healed to get the cast off.

To say I was upset is an understatement. My doctor in Saint John had said nothing about how bad this injury was. I called him when I got back to my parents' place and questioned him. He really didn't have much to say other than he thought I would recover fine from that injury.

He was dead wrong.

I got back to Canada a few weeks later to get my cast off and start my rehab. But things went from bad to worse when I started to see the team physical therapist. I was shocked to see how inept he was. I later found out that those team doctors and therapists were named to their positions mostly because of the checks they wrote to the organization. I quickly changed to a new physical therapist and asked to meet with our team head doctor.

The meeting with the team doctor blew my mind. He told me that he would never send one of his patients to the orthopedic surgeon in Saint John who'd operated on me. He was affectionately known as "the hacker."

I couldn't believe what was going on. I felt powerless.

I called my agent when I got home and was told that he would call me back. Not once in two years had my agent not immediately picked up my call. My frustration was hard to explain. I believed that my agent knew it was a bad injury and was putting me on the back burner. It is amazing how quickly things changed when I got injured.

When I went through the long rehab for my broken femur, I understood the need for patience. The daily monotonous exercises were tough and painful to perform. But they were important, and I needed to just focus on the day and task at hand. It wasn't very different from the daily task of preparing and working out for the season. It just took it one day at a time.

This time, the surgeon told me to expect about a three-month rehab. Because I had done it before, I was confident I would be back for the playoffs when they started in April. The big problem was that the surgery was archaic. Plus, not being able to move the knee joint put me way behind. The muscle in my leg had atrophied, and there was no blood flow going to the tibial plateau fracture. And blood flow is critical in healing an injury.

In this particular instance, I was a very good patient—to a fault. Give me a task, and I will follow it. I knew that I had to power through some pain in rehab. I just didn't realize that I was damaging my knee even further.

I was back skating in late March with the hopes of being ready for the playoffs. But my leg's strength had not fully come back, and there was still a lot of pain in the knee. We ended up going on a deep run in the playoffs, and I desperately wanted to get back. However, the more I pushed, the worse the knee got.

Probably my biggest problem was that I had already rehabbed a broken leg. I assumed that the two injuries were similar in that they were just broken bones. I came to realize that breaking the bone in the knee joint ended up being something completely different.

Our season ended in the conference finals, and I never made it back into the lineup. In hindsight, I should have complained more about the poor care I received, but I was also trying to be a good soldier. Before the injury, I was days away from being called up, and I wanted to stay in the organization's good graces. I tried to stay focused on rehabbing, but it was difficult with the poor care I received in Saint John.

At the end of the season, I flew out to Calgary to visit with the team doctors. I should have gone out there right away, but I didn't know any better. They confirmed the severity of the injury and were puzzled by the problems I was having with my knee. They decided I should have an arthroscopic surgery to look at the knee and clean up anything that could be wrong.

They performed the second surgery and discovered a lot of shredded cartilage that the terrible rehab had probably damaged. They cleaned it up the best they could so I could continue to rehab and get the knee back to the best possible condition in hopes of reviving my career.

Those six to seven months were an absolute nightmare. The initial terrible surgery performed by a team-approved doctor, along with pathetic physical therapy, put me in a bad situation. I did everything I could think of to heal the knee—constant PT, meditation, swimming, biking, supplements, castor oil. I was willing to try anything short of something illegal.

Nothing worked.

The start of training camp was in early September, and I headed back to Calgary to continue my rehab. After a few weeks, camp broke up, and the brass at Calgary decided to send me home for the duration of my rehab. They felt I would be more comfortable going back to my physical therapists at home rather than dealing with the inferior ones in Saint John.

I continued my rehab at home until early February and then flew out to Calgary so the doctors could take a look. After evaluating the knee, they decided I was okay to return to Saint John and continue my playing career. I was still experiencing a lot of pain, but it was time to give it a shot and see if I could withstand the daily grind again.

It was great to get back with the guys, but I was less than thrilled to be back playing for the coach. He had little reaction to me being back, and I just continued to get ready. A few weeks later, I was ready for my first game action in over fourteen months.

Of course, the coach wouldn't make it that simple. He named me to the lineup after a pregame skate early in the day. I was fired up, as were my teammates. I couldn't wait to get back to playing after being off for over a year.

When we went out for the warm-ups, my teammates had me lead the team out to the ice. I couldn't have been any happier at that moment. As we finished the warm-up, one of the assistant coaches pulled me aside in the hallway. He informed me that they were removing me from the lineup for the game. He explained that Calgary had not cleared me to play yet. I knew this was a lie because Calgary had cleared me to play when I was there a few weeks earlier.

The head coach was playing a mind game with me, and I knew it. That night, we had two players who were injured and out of the lineup for the next day's game. When I showed up to the pregame skate the next day, one of the assistant coaches came up to me and told me I was going to be in the lineup that night. I responded that I would not play until the Calgary doctors cleared me.

After practice, I went into the training room to ice my knee. I could see the head coach storming through the locker room. He was pissed that I refused to play. They needed me to play only because we were short players for the night. He entered the training room and proceeded to yell at me for refusing to play.

I snapped and went after him. Players and trainers had to break it up and stop me. He was playing games with my career, and I didn't appreciate it. After the staff and players removed him from the training room, he went back to the coach's office to settle down. After about twenty minutes, he calmly walked back into the training room and asked me if I would play that night if they got a fax from the Calgary doctors clearing me.

I told him yes.

Later that day, I headed back to the rink for the game. They handed me a fax with the doctor's clearance. Finally, this nightmare was over, and I would play my first professional game in fourteen months.

Having persevered through all the bullshit, I went on to score the game-winning goal that night. The team saved the puck for me as a memento. The coach gave a speech to the team after the game, telling everyone how tough I was and how proud he was of me.

What a joke.

The final eighteen games of the season and the playoffs were filled with ups and downs because I couldn't keep the fluid out of my knee. Constant therapy included icing, electronic stimulus, ultrasound, and rehab. Nothing seemed to work.

As a last resort, the doctors put me on an anti-inflammatory medication in an attempt to control the swelling. It instantly worked. I could literally feel the fluid leaving my knee after I took the medication. It was a miracle drug for my career.

By that time, we were heading into the playoffs. I still had up and down days based on the fluid in my knee, but it was more controllable now. We ended up losing in Game 5 of the best-of-five series in the first round of playoffs.

Game 4 was arguably the best game I had as a pro. It was an elimination game that we won in overtime. I had two assists, including one on the winner. I also had probably the best goal of my career. I went end to end and faked out two defensemen before I deked out the goalie. I hit a crossbar and was robbed three other times in the game. It was easily the best I'd felt since my return from the injury.

After we were knocked out of the playoffs, we had one-on-one meetings with the assistant general manager of the Calgary Flames. He told me they wanted me back for another year due to my successful return from the injury. They knew I needed time to keep rehabbing, but he said I was on the right track.

The team flew me and a few other injured players out to Calgary for end-of-the-year physicals. I went through a battery of tests and had a sit-down with the doctors. They were concerned about what they saw in my knee but were encouraged about my overall successful return after fourteen months off. They told me to continue my rehab and that they would see me at training camp.

A few weeks later, my agent called me and asked if I was sitting down. I knew this was not a good sign. He told me that Calgary decided that I had reached my potential and that they were not going to offer me a contract.

This was the worst possible news for my career.

Most teams around the league did not really know me because I had been off for so long. I had been off for fourteen months because Calgary and their approved medical staff had botched my surgery and rehab. And the team had re-signed players who were coming off injury, including my roommate from the year before.

Even though the Calgary doctors passed me on my end-of-year physical, they knew my knee was in bad shape. Calgary simply knew that my full recovery was going to be a long shot and decided to cut bait. Learning that life sometimes isn't fair was a tough lesson to learn at twenty-five. I still had to live life and make a simple choice to stay positive.

Being negative was not going to save my career. Or my life, for that matter.

Chapter 8
Hershey

"It's not the destination. It's the journey."
—Ralph Waldo Emerson

T hat summer, I needed my agent to go out and find a team that would give me a shot to continue my career. He received a lot of interest throughout the summer, but there was no solid deal on the table yet. I was getting frustrated and a little panicked that a deal wouldn't come.

I called him in early August and voiced my frustration that he could not get me a deal. He told me that two things were working against me. First, at twenty-six, I was getting old. But he said that the bigger reason was my time playing in the East Coast Hockey League (ECHL), which was a lower league than the AHL. In the NHL, there was a big stigma against playing below the AHL.

I lost my mind on my agent. I'd never played in the ECHL. He had the wrong Mike Murray. There was another player with my name, and *he'd* played in the ECHL. I couldn't believe that my agent had spent all summer trying to market the wrong person to NHL teams. He quickly backpedaled and said he was mistaken. He insisted that he was not communicating the wrong stats to NHL teams.

I didn't believe him. If he hadn't moved his office from New York City to Colorado the year before, I would have driven straight to his office and voiced my displeasure to his face. The problem was that it was too late in the summer to try to find another agent. I had no choice but to stay with him.

I ended up with a contract with the AHL's Hershey Bears, which was one of the longest-running teams in the league. It also had a great history. Gordie Howe, who was selected into the Hockey Hall of Fame in 1972 and was known as Mr. Hockey, once remarked, "Everybody who is anybody in hockey has played in Hershey." It was one of my favorite places to play in the AHL. It had a great rink and die-hard fans. I was pumped to continue my career in such a historic place.

Hershey was the top farm team for the Colorado Avalanche. Bob Hartley was the head coach, and he had led them to the Calder Cup Championship the prior season. It was a great opportunity to revive my career.

The knee was still giving me trouble, but I was able to build a lot of strength back in my leg over the summer. I headed into camp confident that my knee would hold up. The first day of camp, we did some off-ice testing. This was where my plans started to unravel.

One of the tests was a shuttle run. We were in a basketball gym and had to continuously run back and forth between two markers. It was a short but intense test and was not great for my knee. I let them know that I needed to sit out the test because of my knee. That sent up a red flag to the medical and coaching staff.

I naturally assumed that because Calgary had passed me on my end-of-the-year physical only a few months earlier, my knee wouldn't be an issue in Hershey.

I was wrong. They sent me for an X-ray early the next day before the first on-ice practice.

I arrived at practice in time to get on the ice. Fully dressed in my new Hershey Bears uniform, I headed down the hallway to get on the ice. On the way, the head coach and general manager asked to talk to me in the coach's office.

They sat me down and explained that I had failed my physical. The team doctors looked at the X-rays and decided there was too much damage for them to put me out on the ice without having me sign a waiver. The coach and general manager were pretty nice about it. They told me to call my agent from the coach's office and talk it over with him. They stepped out, and I made the call.

When I explained the situation to my agent, he immediately told me not to sign the waiver. Instead, he instructed me to return to my hotel room and call him back. I hung up and told the coach and general manager that I needed to think about it before making a final decision. They were understanding and told me to take my time.

When I got back to the hotel, I called my agent. He was able to arrange a call between me and the doctor who'd evaluated me. The doctor gave me some sobering news about the risk of continuing my career. What I remember most is him saying that if I wanted to play with my kids one day, I should give up playing professional hockey. He concluded that, based on his brief evaluation, my knee was beyond repair.

This took the wind out of my sails. It was crushing news, but I couldn't completely disagree with it. I had spent the last twenty months trying to get my knee back to normal, and nothing was working. I decided to leave the Hershey camp and return home to ponder my future. It wasn't the outcome and great opportunity I'd expected.

Once I got home, I did a lot of thinking for a few weeks. I talked with my family, Joy, and my agent, as well as a few other doctors. The consensus was to retire. The writing was on the wall, and the wisdom of taking their collective advice and moving on with my life was pretty obvious.

Even though the situation was beyond my control, I could control the outcome. I didn't regret the effort that I'd put into the endless rehab to continue my career. The frustration, the pain, and the bad advice were simply beyond my control. During those months of rehab, I'd been able to do only the best I could do. I didn't beat myself up over the what-ifs.

I'd been a good soldier and trusted the people around me. Most of them had my best interests in mind. Maybe, in hindsight, I could have taken a step back and raised my hand. I could have asked whether I had the absolute best surgeon to do my operation. Maybe I could have asked for a second opinion. That is easy to say now. At that moment, though,

I had to trust that Calgary had the best doctors in place to do my surgery. I had to trust that my trainer had consulted the Calgary brass and that they had approved the surgery. I felt powerless at the time. I don't regret how I handled the situation. I feel that I didn't leave a stone unturned in trying to revive my career.

It was definitely strange to not have hockey to focus on. Over the last ten years, I had been on a mission to live out my dreams of playing hockey in the NHL. Trying to figure out what to do with my life in my new reality was a bigger challenge than I ever thought it would be.

As tough as it was, I still wanted to enjoy my life. I reconnected with old friends and spent more time with Joy. I enjoyed the holidays more than I had since high school. I made a conscious decision to be happy instead of mad. To be honest, it was a lot more exhausting being mad. I chose to be happy.

To say I wasn't ready to give up on hockey would be a major understatement. It was the first time in over twenty years that I was not playing the sport that I loved and that defined me. Throughout most of my year away from it, I pondered what to do with my life. It isn't easy to make a major shift in your life when you are not completely ready.

Toward the end of the winter, I started helping an old college teammate with the hockey camps that he started operating after he graduated from college. I demonstrated various skating edge-control drills, along with exercises focused on stick handling and shooting. We were on the ice for three hours, with different age groups cycling through every hour. I was able to get myself out on the ice again and put a little extra money in my pocket. Plus, it was a bit of a distraction from solely focusing on what to do with my life.

I had been rehabbing the knee throughout the year just to improve my overall quality of life. To my surprise, when I got on the ice again, my knee felt a lot better than I'd anticipated. To be clear, the knee was crap, and that was not going to change. But it felt a lot better compared to how it felt when I retired in September. And it got me thinking about possibly playing again. If I could learn how to deal with the pain, I thought maybe I could give it another shot.

It was tough to get that far in my career and be so close to the NHL, then walk away without any second thoughts. I knew that returning was a long shot, but I did not want to regret not trying everything possible to return to the ice. I knew that one day, I was going to be too old to play at that level. You see, there is a clock in sports, and that buzzer will go off eventually. I just didn't want to be the one to push the button.

I decided to go all in again and give it one last shot. Call me crazy, but for my sanity, I needed to give it one last try. I continued to rehab and skate in the spring and summer. I also followed a rigorous workout schedule to get into the best shape I could.

I started skating with area professionals at Providence College that summer. I ran into an old assistant college coach of mine who was scouting in the International Hockey League (IHL) with the Cincinnati Cyclones. He was able to get me a tryout with the Cyclones. There were no guarantees—just a chance. I left for Cincinnati in early September.

Chapter 9
Louisiana

"Our greatest weakness lies in giving up.
The most certain way to succeed is always
to try just one more time."

–Thomas A. Edison

C incinnati was an independent team in the IHL and had affiliations with a couple of NHL teams for players. I had a very solid camp. Before it ended on Friday, the team notified me that they wanted to sign me to a one-year contract. By the time Monday came, the Ottawa Senators sent two of their players down to the Cyclones. Both clubs agreed to split the two players' salaries, effectively getting two players for the price of one.

My agent called me on Monday to tell me that the terms of the contract were changing. The team now wanted to sign me to a two-way contract with their ECHL affiliate in Dayton, Ohio. I gave them a hard "Thanks, but no thanks." If I was going to play at a lower level, it was not going to be in Dayton, Ohio. No offense. I ended up deciding to go home and think about my next move.

While I was at camp, I met a player, Blair Manning, who was also there on a tryout. He already had an ECHL contract with the Louisiana IceGators in Lafayette, Louisiana. This was a backup in case he wasn't offered a contract in Cincinnati. He had already signed a contract with the IceGators and told me how unbelievable it was to play in Lafayette. It was hard to believe, to be honest. They owned their own private bus that had bunks, satellite TV, refrigerators, etc. Also, the fans were crazy dedicated. They were selling out the eleven-thousand-seat Cajundome and were the hottest ticket in town.

After a few days at home, a former teammate from Umass–Lowell, Don Parsons, called me. He had been playing down in Louisiana for a couple years and heard from Blair that I was back playing. He connected me with his coach, Doug Shedden, who sold me on the reasons for making the trek. I was skeptical at first, as I was contemplating giving up hockey for good. For the first two weeks in Cincinnati, my knee was pretty good. But it had started to act up again in the last few days. I thought about it, talked with my family, and decided to give it one last try. I figured I could close that chapter by giving it a chance and, if it didn't work out, at least have some peace of mind.

When I talked with the coach about the salary, and I thought he was joking. They would pay me $350 per week, but, by finding me other outside work with local businesses, he would make me one of the highest-paid guys on the team. These were not guarantees but a common practice for many teams in the league. This was all foreign to me because I was coming off a three-year NHL contract, and everything was spelled out in the contract. I circled back with Donnie, who assured me it would be worth the trip. I thought I could go down for two weeks and have some fun. If it didn't work out, I could hang up my skates and go home. I really had nothing to lose.

It would turn out to be one of the best decisions of my life.

I flew down to Lafayette, met with the coach, and discussed my contract. Because I had played three seasons in the AHL, which is a league higher than the ECHL, he was willing to pay me at the higher end of the team. The only problem was that the ECHL had a hard weekly salary cap. To fit my pay within the salary cap, he wanted to pay me the $350 per week.

When I was playing in the AHL under an NHL contract I was paid $60,000 for the twenty-six weeks. That was $2,307 per week. Dropping down to $350 per week was $9,100 for the twenty-six weeks. The majority of players that were coming off an NHL contract would command more in weekly salary from the ECHL.

I was willing to take less money because I had taken the prior year off. I was just happy to be back playing, and money was not my concern.

Even though the Louisiana IceGators played in the lower ECHL, some players made more money than they did under an NHL contract. There were many other ways in which we were compensated. First, housing was free of charge. Some players owned houses that the team paid for, but most had apartments or condos that the team paid for. Companies could hire you for marketing opportunities to make additional compensation.

All utilities except phone and cable were paid, but I quickly learned that even those could be negotiated. The team rented all our furniture, including washer and dryer. They also had several deals in town with local restaurants and bars where we would eat and drink for free. Believe me, NHL contracts were great, and players on big teams could make a lot of money. However, for many players in the minors, the ECHL was more profitable.

My first year in Lafayette couldn't have gone better. We had the best team in the league, and the Cajun fans were incredible. They treated us like royalty. *Time* magazine even wrote an article about us being the most successful minor league team of all time. My plan to go down for a few weeks to have fun and then retire quickly changed after my first home game.

We came out to a sold-out crowd, as close to twelve thousand fans packed the Cajundome. I was hooked after that game. I had never been a part of a team like that before. I called Joy and told her that she better make plans to move to Lafayette because I wasn't coming home anytime soon.

The people in Lafayette were incredible hosts, and, to my surprise, the hockey was a lot better than I'd anticipated.

We had a weekly radio show on Monday nights that we were required to attend, meals were routinely dropped off at our houses, and we could barely ever buy our own drinks. After every home game, we were required to go to a post-game party at a local restaurant. All the food and drinks were free, and fans cheered for us as we entered. It was surreal. Throw on top of it a free golf membership, and I was hooked.

My ultimate goal was always to play in the NHL. But I realized at this point that if some medical miracle didn't happen to cure my knee, I would never attain that goal. I just couldn't train anymore like I had before my knee was destroyed. My dedication to training had always been my calling card as an athlete. I felt that I trained harder than most, especially when no one else was watching.

Now, unfortunately, my ace in the hole was gone. But this was not going to stop me from competing. I still think I played at a high level. I just wasn't as consistent anymore. I had good days and bad days that I couldn't control. Playing at a slightly lower level allowed me to take days off when I needed to. Teams didn't allow that at the higher level.

Finally, when I got to Lafayette, I was exposed to a new anti-inflammatory medication called Vioxx. It worked miracles and was the only thing that kept fluid out of my knee. I could ice twenty-four hours a day, and it wouldn't have mattered. The medication was, without a doubt, the reason I was able to play three more years.

What a three years it would be.

Year One

The first year in Louisiana was the best of the three. We had a great team with a coach who wanted to work hard and play hard. It was the team's fourth year in Lafayette. After that year, the interest in the team slowly declined. But when I arrived, we were still treated like rock stars. We had all the benefits and money that they'd had in the previous years. We had a great team and finished the year as the President Cup winners as the best team in the league.

The main difference between the ECHL and the higher leagues was that the ECHL had really good players with some faults in their game. Maybe they weren't fast enough or big enough. Some players were highly skilled but at the end of their careers. Some just had poor habits. In any case, there were still some highly competitive games. I enjoyed being able to compete at a high level without the stress of the day-to-day grind of the AHL and IHL.

Throughout the year, I got better acclimated to the league and adjusted to my cranky knee. On numerous occasions, IHL teams came calling, looking for my services. I declined them all because I was enjoying playing hockey for the first time in three to four years. I felt that I had already proven myself at that higher level. The only way I needed to be in the IHL was if the NHL was a realistic shot. I knew that my knee was not good enough to compete at that level, so I decided it was best to stay down in the ECHL and enjoy the moment.

Joy was getting acclimated to Lafayette and had found a job at a local law firm. The people of Lafayette were extremely welcoming to us, and we fit into the community very quickly. We settled into our new apartment and could not have been happier.

There always seemed to be some sort of party going on in the city. There were crawfish boils, post-game parties, New Year's Eve bashes, Mardi Gras events, and pool parties after practice. It didn't hurt that there were drive-thru daiquiri huts on corners like there were Dunkin Donuts at home. The difference was that the daiquiri huts served alcohol in two-gallon jugs.

The year ended with a first-round upset to the New Orleans Brass. There's nothing you can do when you outshoot a team 65–12 in the deciding game and lose 3–2. It was a tough way to end a season in which we thought we were going to win the Kelly Cup and be the champions of the ECHL.

Unfortunately, my coach convinced me to sign a playoff contract with the IHL's Manitoba Moose in case we were knocked out early. Little did I know I would be on a plane to Canada the day after our season ended. Leaving eighty-degree weather to fly into a snowstorm in Manitoba, Canada, was not my idea of the perfect ending to my first season in Louisiana.

After being in Canada for a few days, I learned that my hometown team, the Providence Bruins, had called, looking for me to join them in the AHL playoffs. That was a real bummer. It was no big deal, though. It wasn't like they were going to win the championship that year anyway.

One morning, I was walking into the team locker room when the coach pulled me aside and said that my buddy, John Spoltore (Spotty), who had been called up to Providence, scored the overtime winner in their first-round series. Now, I could write a whole book about Spotty, so it didn't surprise me that he would score an overtime winner like that. But there was no doubt that I was a little jealous that he played for my hometown team. I just had to laugh at the circumstances.

When I walked into the locker room the very next morning, the coach informed me that Spotty scored the overtime winner the night before. I told him that he'd already told me that. He laughed and said Spotty had done it again. He went on to score three overtime winners in that series while I was stuck in the press box in Winnipeg.

We ended up winning our first round against Milwaukee and then went on to lose to Chicago. I spent a total of three weeks with the Moose and never got a chance to play. At least I got to pocket a little money before summer started.

By the time I went home to Rhode Island, the Providence Bruins were in the finals of the Calder Cup. John Spoltore was the team's leading scorer but never got to play in the finals. The Boston Bruins sent a bunch of their prospects down to Providence after they were eliminated from the NHL playoffs. Providence went on to win the Calder Cup, and I went and partied with Spotty and the team all that night.

That summer, I was drafted in the ninth round by the Dallas Stallions of Roller Hockey International, which was a professional inline hockey league. I tried to convince Joy to go to Dallas for the summer, and she politely declined. It was a little tougher when Las Vegas traded for my rights halfway through the summer and used incentives to pressure me to go. That still got a no from Joy. Quite honestly, I didn't really want to go anyway. I needed the time off for my knee so I could get ready for the upcoming season.

I had a few options over that summer to go to England or Germany for the following season. But Louisiana came to me with an offer that was tough to walk away from. Only a few players were offered year-round contracts that came with full medical and the chance to go back to the city that I loved playing in. It was tough to walk away from the security and hospitality.

Year Two

Joy and I moved back to Lafayette in early September, and, right away, things were very different. Our coach had been fired, and the team decided to hire a general manager who lived in Toronto and a coach who had never coached before. The team was mainly the same, but the vibe was very different from the year before. We started off on the road for the first two weeks, and things were not going well.

The new coach had never coached before, and it showed. He had been a rookie superstar for the New York Rangers in the late '70s but made a series of poor choices that left him out of the NHL. He bounced around organizations until he got his first coaching gig. It was a joke, and I didn't take too kindly to it. I was a process guy, and he had none at all. There was no scouting report and no team meetings. The assistant coach ran the practices. The coach seemed to be a figurehead and would just go out and party every night.

A month or so into the season, the team was struggling. The coach called me into his office and told me I had been traded to the Augusta Lynx. I laughed at him and told him if he thought I was the problem on the team, he had no idea what he was doing. Which was obviously the case.

I told them there was no way I was reporting to Augusta. I decided to drive home with Joy and figure out my next move. One reason I refused to report was that I was in a lawsuit against the trainer in Augusta. He had been my trainer in Saint John when I broke my tibial plateau and was part of the group of people whose advice led me to have to retire from hockey. Most of my issues were with the team doctors, the physical therapist, and the Calgary Flames. The trainer didn't have a lot to do with it. But, nonetheless, he was involved. It would have been super awkward to play in Augusta with him in the trainer's room.

Another reason was that if I was going to play in the ECHL, I was going to dictate the terms. I loved playing in Lafayette, and I loved my teammates. The only way I was going to play somewhere else was if the money was comparable and the situation was similar. That was very tough to find with any other team.

I ended up going home for a little over a month and enjoyed the Thanksgiving holiday with my family and friends. During my time away from Lafayette, the team continued to struggle. The president of the IceGators called me on a regular basis, trying to convince me to accept the trade to Augusta and report to the team. I refused. He actually told me that I would report as soon as I started having money problems. I laughed at him and let him know that was why I went to college. I could just retire again and get a job. I was playing for fun and was not going to get into a situation I didn't want to be in.

The other problem that Louisiana was having in trading me was that I was guaranteed money in the form of paid expenses and appearance fees. They didn't want anyone to know and played dumb when I confronted them with my issues about being traded. I was on a year-round contract, and they were paying me these added incentives. Augusta had no idea about this arrangement, and they were certainly not going to pay me the extra money. But I was not going to let Louisiana off the hook.

As the team continued to struggle, some key players went to ownership and insisted that they trade back for me. We had a great group of veterans, and they knew what I meant to the team. The coaches and the general manager had no idea what was going on. They actually perceived me as a problem and didn't realize that I was a team-first guy who had the entire team's respect.

Sometime in early December, the president of the team called me and asked me if I would come back if they traded for me. I told him I would, but only if they put my incentives agreement in writing. He reluctantly agreed, and I wrote a contract with the team. Believe me, that doesn't happen every day.

I came back to the team in December and couldn't have been happier. Joy joined me right after the holidays. I don't think the coaching staff wanted me back, but I really didn't care. The team wanted me back, and that was all I cared about.

As soon as we got the band back together, we started to get back to our winning ways. We finished near the top of our league and were primed to take another run at the Kelly Cup. I was hoping we had learned our lesson from the previous year.

As I continued to play hockey at this level, I learned some lessons that I wished I had learned earlier. These are things you can see at the highest levels of hockey to this day, particularly in playoffs: the importance of playing to the final buzzer, enjoying the moment, and staying in the moment.

I made a conscious decision to have a different mindset as we headed into the playoffs. More often than not, I performed well in these situations. But I wanted to be better. I wanted to always strive for consistency. I got very hyped for games, and, for the most part, it worked. On some occasions, I got too hyped and came out with no energy.

I decided that instead of listening to hard rock music and being overly serious, I would change it up. I listened to feel-good music and came in with a smile on my face, feeling as loose as I could while also being serious. No matter the situation, I pretended it was the best day of my life.

Before games, I would not think ahead to the game at all. I already knew what to do. I stayed in the moment and distracted myself anytime I thought ahead to the game. It wasn't easy, but the more I did this, the more energy I played with and the more consistent I became. It paid huge dividends in the weeks ahead.

Our first-round opponents were the Mississippi Sea Wolves. We were taken to a deciding game and ended up winning when I scored a last-minute goal to put us ahead. We beat the Pee Dee Pride in the second round and faced the Greenville Growl in the Southern Conference Championship.

We headed to Greenville, South Carolina, to play the first two games of the series. Even though we had a very good team, Greenville was better. They were deeper and more talented than we were that year. In the first game, we got out to a quick lead and were up 3–1 into the third period. Greenville was relentless and eventually came back to beat us 4–3.

Game 2 was a classic playoff battle between two tough teams that went back and forth into overtime. We ended up losing in quadruple overtime. It was the longest game in ECHL history. The marathon game did not end until two a.m. and lasted a total of 121:24.

It was an emotional, crushing defeat for us. Being down 2–0 to that very talented team seemed like an insurmountable task. On top of that, we had to hop on a bus and travel seven hundred and fifty miles back to Lafayette, which took us over twelve hours. Believe it or not, we had to play Game 3 only twelve hours later.

Our coach told us that twenty years later, we would be sitting somewhere having a beer and talking to someone about this hockey game and how we'd played in one of the longest games in hockey history and lost. And that was not the end of the story. I realized twenty years later that he was exactly right.

It's funny because, around the same time, the Philadelphia Flyers went to an epic five overtimes and won against the Pittsburgh Penguins. As we watched ESPN's coverage of that game, our team couldn't help but laugh at how tough the Flyers were to play another game two days later after staying in luxury hotels, getting an extra day off, and having the best food and medical staff. They got pretty much anything they needed to be ready to play in two days.

What we had to do was absolutely ridiculous, but it was an unbelievable experience. Many of us could barely get on the bus. Some guys were dehydrated, there were ice bags everywhere, and we didn't have the greatest food to refuel. Several of us took IV fluids on the way back. Sleep on a bus is not the best, and I didn't get much of it.

We ended up getting back into Lafayette around one p.m. the next day. We had to be back at the rink by five p.m. for the seven p.m. game time. We all limped off the bus and couldn't believe that we had to play that night. Girlfriends and wives met us in the parking lot to get us home.

When I barely managed to get in Joy's car, I could only muster up a few words: "Chicken parm and ice." She knew exactly what I meant, dropped me off at the apartment, and went out to get everything.

I walked in the apartment and just collapsed on the couch. About thirty minutes later, she came in with the food and about five bags of ice. I got myself up to start eating. Joy then filled up the tub with the ice so it would be ready when I finished the chicken parm.

After finishing about thirty minutes later, I made my way to the bathroom. I undressed, climbed into a tub of absolutely bone-chilling water, and submerged myself. For about two to three minutes, I was in excruciating pain, moaning and clenching my fist to combat it. After about three minutes, I went totally numb. I sat there for about ten minutes until I was cooked.

After getting dressed, I made my way to the bedroom. I looked at Joy and asked her to get me up a little after four p.m. Then I collapsed again and passed out for a couple of hours. Around four, I awoke, reluctantly got up, and looked at Joy in disbelief.

As I got ready for the game, I looked in the mirror and thought, *How can I possibly play tonight?* I had never felt that bad in my entire life. I was shaky, dehydrated, and exhausted. I left the room, looked at Joy, and said I had no idea how I was going to play. It was the worst I'd felt physically and mentally in my entire life. I could not wait for the game to be over so I could get back in bed.

On my way over to the rink, I had some time to think. I had to reach deep into my memory bank and remember times when I'd had to deal with something similar. The first thing that came to mind was the Culver Military Academy game in prep school. I felt so terrible in that game, and all I could do was focus one moment at a time. For about four hours, I refused to think about anything else other than breathing.

It worked. That prep school game was one of the best games of my life. It was the game that got me drafted into the NHL. I decided I had to use the same methodology. So, when I arrived at the rink, I just focused on my breathing. Took another ice bath, a bag of IV fluid, stretches, getting my sticks ready, the team warm-up, the team meeting, and then the game itself, I focused on my breathing. Anytime my thoughts drifted, I went back to that.

I was so focused that before I knew it, the game was over. We ended up winning in overtime and changed the direction of the seven-game series. I scored a goal and an assist, and I played one of my best games of the playoffs. It is amazing what the body can accomplish when the mind is completely focused. It was truly a pivotal moment in shaping how I think about performance in games. That is what we are ultimately judged on—the game.

We went on to win Games 4 and 5 at home. We could see the tide turn and the look of defeat in Greenville's eyes. We were relentless, and they started to not believe they could win. Game 6 went back to Greenville, and we ended up finishing the series four games to two. That was four straight wins after the incredibly tough start to the series. It was one of the best moments and memories of my career.

Next up was the Northern Conference Champion, the Peoria Rivermen, for the Kelly Cup. They were the farm team of the St. Louis Blues and had a very talented group. We rode the bus for fourteen hours to Peoria, Illinois, a few days before the finals to play Games 1 and 2.

For our teams, playing for a professional championship was not much different than playing for the Stanley Cup. Obviously, the NHL players were better than us, but we wanted our cup as much as they wanted theirs. We went through the same grind they did: a seven-game series, travel, injuries, great wins, and tough losses. Everyone was putting everything on the line.

We got off to a fast start and won the first two games of the series. Every game was a grind and could have gone either way. We went back to Lafayette for Games 3, 4, and 5. We had not lost at home in more than twenty-five games. We were heavy favorites to win the cup at home.

Game 3 was a back-and-forth battle. In the middle of the second period, with the game tied, a forward on Peoria collided with our goalie. Our goalie ended up dislocating his elbow, which knocked him out for the rest of the finals. It was a tough blow. The one position that can win you a championship is the goalie. He was playing unbelievably well, and it was tough on the backup to go in without having played in about two months.

Things went downhill for us pretty fast. We went to overtime and lost on a shot from behind our net that bounced in off the back of our goalie's leg. We could see the momentum changing just like it did in our games against Greenville in the series before. We ended up losing the next two games and went back to Peoria for the next game.

Game 6 was another battle that went into overtime. We quickly took a penalty and went on the penalty kill. A minute or so into the power play, Peoria scored and ended our season. It was crushing. To watch that team celebrate the championship in front of us after we'd had the series under control was a brutal way to end.

I finished as one of the leading scorers in the playoffs. In nineteen games, I had eleven goals and nine assists for twenty points. It was an incredible run that we just couldn't finish. So many things that I learned to be a successful player when it mattered most in the biggest games of the season. Unfortunately, I left the playoffs with a partially torn labrum in my shoulder—something I had to play with throughout the playoff run. Most of my teammates and competitors likely had similar challenges. It was part of the deal, but it was definitely taking its toll on me.

Year Three

I took a little time after the season was done to decide whether I was going to return for another season. I still felt I had some gas left in the tank and that my love of the game was still there. Quite honestly, that love was rekindled when I first arrived in Louisiana. Probably like most athletes, I didn't want it to end.

Louisiana was the only place where I wanted to continue my career. The greatest decision I ever made was to come out of retirement and give hockey one more shot. If my career had ended in Hershey, Pennsylvania, I think I always would have regretted it. True to my mantra since senior year in high school, I didn't want to regret not doing everything possible to continue my career and see if I could still make the NHL.

I was at peace with how my career had turned out. I knew I'd done everything possible to continue playing and didn't regret it one bit. I still wasn't done playing, but I knew the knee would never hold up to the grind of playing at the AHL/ NHL level. I could just play and love every single minute of it. It didn't matter to me that I was playing at a lower level. I could still compete and have the feeling of being really good at something.

There were times in my days in Lafayette when my knee felt really good. On those days, I felt like an NHL player. I was unstoppable, and that feeling was addicting. The reality is that those days were fewer and far between. It didn't, however, overtake my love of the game and my enjoyment of the moment.

During my last year in Louisiana, we had another great team. But the aura around the team had changed. A new coaching staff came in and changed the vibe of the organization. It was more professional and less like *Varsity Blues*. The arena had fewer and fewer fans. The perks we received slowly went away, and the money was drying up. The ownership group seemed less engaged.

We had another great regular season, but it ended like the previous seasons. We ended up losing in the Southern Conference Finals to the South Carolina Stingrays in six games. That ended three of the greatest years of my life, leaving me with incredible memories and absolutely no regrets.

A few weeks after the season was over, Joy and I got married. We took the summer to figure out what our next steps would be. I still felt I could play another year. I'd been courted by a few teams in England and Germany over the last few years, and I thought it would be nice to start my marriage and end my career by playing one year in Europe.

Not too long after our wedding as the summer came to an end, everything we knew as normal changed. And it would be the end of my career.

Chapter 10
The Case

"'Tis better to have loved and lost than
never to have loved at all."
—Alfred Lord Tennyson

I woke up on September 11, 2001, like I did any normal day.
I got up early and dropped Joy at the train to take her trip
into Boston for work. My routine was to go to the gym and get
my workout in for the day. I was still in professional hockey
mode and was planning to head to Europe by the end of the
month.

By the time I got back to my parents' house, everything
had changed forever.

The tragic day of 9/11 changed the world forever. When
I got home from the gym, my brother Kevin was at the house
dropping something off for our dad. They yelled at me to come
over to the TV and watch what was going on. Two planes had
slammed into the World Trade Center. It was obvious that it

was a terror attack. Our attention immediately turned to my older brother Bill, who worked on Wall Street.

My father was able to get him on the phone. He was safe and sound for the moment in his office. He assured us that everything was fine and that they were sitting around waiting for instructions as to what to do. He told us he would keep us updated and hung up the phone.

As we sat watching the TV within the hour of the attack, we noticed something major happening. We almost couldn't believe it. There was a huge cloud of dust, and it appeared that the building had collapsed. Sure enough, that was exactly what happened. It never even occurred to us at the time that the buildings could come down. My dad called my brother, but this time, he got nothing.

We spent the better part of the day trying to get him, but cell service had been cut off. Unbeknownst to us, my brother had decided to leave his building and go to the Dunkin Donuts across the street while he was waiting for instructions. After Bill grabbed his coffee, he stepped outside as the first Twin Tower building, which was only a few blocks away, came down. It seemed like Armageddon to him. Most of the people around him thought they were under attack again. They all ran toward the river to avoid all the dust and ash.

My brother eventually found his way back to his building by touching the exterior walls of buildings to feel his way. No one could see anything due to all the dust. Bill gathered his things and left the building. He, along with thousands of people, walked all the way to Long Island. We didn't hear from him to learn he was safe until later in the day.

I know it had a deep impact on him and the rest of my family. It was pretty clear that America was going to war very soon. Life as we knew it would never be the same. Everyone old enough on 9/11 knows exactly where they were that day. Like many people, I now look at my life as before 9/11 and after 9/11.

After a few weeks of thinking, I unceremoniously decided it was the end of my career. At that time, I felt it was the right thing to do, and I have no regrets over it. I had spent a long time pursuing this dream, and maybe I could have squeaked out another year or two of my playing career. But it seemed kind of pointless. I didn't want to be thirty hours by car or eight hours by plane away from my family anymore. I especially didn't want to move Joy over to Europe and put us in jeopardy. I didn't feel it would be safe to take her overseas. I didn't want us to be a target in a country where we couldn't protect ourselves.

It was time to move on and put down some roots back where I grew up. It was a pretty easy decision at the time. There was only one thing that I had to tie up before I could move on with my life away from hockey: the lawsuit I'd filed in Canada after it became clear that the treatment I had received contributed to the irreparable damage to my knee. The first hearing for the lawsuit was a little over a year away, and I still had to live my new life. But it was difficult to move on until the lawsuit was over.

In August of 2002, five years after filing my lawsuit, I was just days away from my first formal court hearing. The legal system works a lot differently in Canada, but I was confident in the counsel I had chosen. George Byrne was someone I had come to trust and respect as he helped guide me through this process.

I had the opportunity to spend a week with George and his family the summer before the trial because of the discovery process that I had to go through. This cemented my trust and confidence in him. He had a great wife and three wonderful children. George and I had spent many grueling days in a conference room while I was interrogated—sorry, "deposed"—by the defendant's lawyers and nights watching baseball and getting to know each other. I had entrusted my story to him. And, in some respect, I was trusting him to protect the small legacy I had created for myself. It had taken an incredible amount of pride to try to accomplish my lifelong dream of playing hockey at its highest level.

None of those dreams had ended with me suing my former team and the doctors they had selected for me. The incompetence of doctors and therapists they had forced upon me had stolen my ability to play hockey. Now I was finally going to be able to tell my story and get on with my life. Five days and counting before I headed up to Canada.

I spent the prior weekend with my family. We had cousins in town, and my older sister, Debbie, was hosting everyone at her house for a cookout. I left early on Sunday to meet my father, brother, and cousin for a round of golf before the cookout. We had a great day with lots of laughs and competition. No doubt,

I was a little anxious about my upcoming week, and this was the perfect distraction. After the round, we went over to my sister's place to join the rest of the family.

The majority of my family and some cousins I had not seen in a while were enjoying the day as well. Even though I had a stressful week ahead, I was excited to tell my cousins about the new job I had started that summer. It was the first job I'd gotten after my pro hockey career. It had been difficult to move ahead with life after hanging up my skates, and I was finally looking to close that chapter and move forward.

When we arrived at the house, Joy was anxious to talk with me. I hardly noticed, what with all the family around and catching up. She eventually was able to grab my attention and asked me to take a walk. I thought it was a little odd, considering all the people there, many of whom we hadn't seen in quite some time, but I agreed.

As we walked down the street, I could see that she was trembling. I immediately turned to her and asked what was wrong. She took a deep breath and said, "I have some bad news."

"Well, what is it?"

She told me George Byrne had accidently drowned on his last day of vacation. He'd gone out for the last swim of the day with his brother and nephew and been caught in a riptide.

I couldn't believe what I was hearing. I was in complete shock. A lawyer in his firm had contacted Joy to pass along the devastating news. I had no idea what to do. Cry, scream, smash something? We just stood there and hugged for about fifteen minutes. All I could think of was his wife and kids.

Joy told me that the lawyers still wanted me to go up to Canada and continue with the settlement conference that Thursday. My initial reaction was no, and I wanted to drop the whole case. It seemed meaningless in light of this news. I ended up taking the next several days to discuss it with Joy and my parents. I also had a few phone conversations with the lawyers from George's firm who were taking over my case.

After several long days of talking and thinking over what I should do, I came to a decision. I would go through with the settlement conference. The lawyers assured me that this was what George would have wanted and that they were up to speed with the case. I was extremely conflicted but eventually decided maybe this was the best for everyone involved. If I won, George's family would receive a little money. And I could finally move on with my life.

Man, this sucked!

Joy and I decided to leave a day early and drive up to attend the funeral in Saint John. We didn't want to tell anyone that we were going because we didn't want to be a distraction for his family. We arrived at the funeral and took a seat in the back. It was jam-packed and emotional, to say the least. The mass lasted about an hour.

After paying our respects, we quietly left and checked into our hotel. As we were settling into our room, the phone rang. I answered and was surprised to hear our new lawyer's voice. He asked if we had attended the funeral.

He was asking because George's wife, Margo, wanted to speak to me. Immediately, that sense of panic washed over me. Why, on this day, did she want to speak to me? Of course, I would speak to her, but it was an intimidating moment. What would I say? What did she want to say? It would take me until our last day in Saint John a few days later to finally meet with her.

We settled into our room and tried to relax for a little bit. The new lawyers wanted to meet us at their office in the early evening to go over what would transpire the next day. There was a lot of buildup to that settlement conference. I was anxious and no doubt conflicted about getting through it.

We met for about an hour with the two lawyers who were taking over. They assured me that they were deeply involved in the case and were confident about how it would be handled. We had a pretty good case with strong evidence of neglect and liability on our side. A doctor out of Toronto was our expert witness. And we felt that a reasonable person would be able to see that my care had not been handled properly and had led to the premature ending of my career.

As we went through the case, the lawyers were very confident that I wouldn't walk out of there without less than $1 million. The suit was for over $4 million, but they felt I would receive at least $1 million. They told me that this type of money would forever change my life and my family's life. This was overwhelming news to us, but it was what we were hoping for. We left the office both elated and conflicted about the news they'd just given us.

After the meeting, we went to Vito's, which was one of my favorite restaurants in Saint John. We quietly sat there and enjoyed my favorite meal: Chicken Vito's Style, with a bucket of mussels. Joy and I just looked at each other in stunned silence. To receive such devastating news a few days earlier with such great news now was overwhelming. I had pretty big superstitions, so we didn't really talk about it all that much. But it was hard not to dream about the possibilities.

We had just gotten married in June and were low on funds after paying for the wedding and spending money on the case. We were anxious to move forward in our lives, buy a house, and set ourselves up for the future. As we settled down in bed before the big day, I realized that I would be in for a restless night.

The next morning, we headed over to our lawyers' office to meet before heading to the settlement conference. They had concerned looks on their faces as we entered and were completely blindsided by the news they shared. They had spent most of the night going over the case and reached out to our expert witness. He was getting cold feet about testifying against the doctors. It seemed like George's absence or a reluctance to testify against fellow doctors had got to him.

Not having George to talk with the doctor and hold him to his commitment to testify put us in an extremely difficult spot. The strength of our case was based heavily on his opinion. We had to decide whether we should go on with the case or postpone it and find a new expert witness. Our new lawyers felt we still could have a strong case and to continue with the settlement conference.

After taking a moment privately, Joy and I decided that the best option was to move forward with the case. We had been through too much in the last five years and, more importantly, the last few days to postpone it. I didn't quite have the energy to postpone and go through another year of waiting. I also couldn't help feeling conflicted over continuing with this case; here I was talking about a lawsuit, and George was gone. He had lost his life, and his kids had lost their father. How could I be upset if the dollar amount wasn't what I'd hoped?

We walked into the courtroom and immediately saw a few of the parties to the suit. It had been five years since the last time I'd seen them. It was a very awkward experience to sit next to the people I felt ruined my career. In my opinion, most of these individuals had been completely in over their heads in treating professional athletes. They never should have been put in that situation and were likely hired without proper vetting. It was probably a political hire or out of convenience.

The conference lasted about five hours. Toward the end, the judge asked to speak with our team privately in his chambers. He was an older man, probably in his late sixties. He was a former athlete who was actually against playing sports at the pro level. He thought players were putting their bodies at too great a risk for their future. It was hard for me to disagree with him, given my present and undoubtedly future problems that I will face with my damaged knee.

We talked at length about what it would take to move this case forward to trial, and the risks involved. In Canada, if you lose a civil suit, the defendants can, in return, sue you for hundreds of thousands of dollars in legal fees. This unquestionably made me nervous. I barely had any money as it was and certainly didn't want to risk my future or my family's. Plus, with the loss of our expert witness, it was a big risk to move forward with the lawsuit and find another doctor to testify on my behalf.

The judge pointed out the positives of moving on with my life. It was an incredibly tough decision.

It was just a day after George Byrne's funeral, and I was without question looking at the case through different eyes. I didn't really have the relationship or confidence in my new lawyers to let them advise me or know what was in my best interest. It seemed to us that they just wanted to close this case and tie up some loose ends as a result of George's death. George had handled my case for five years; they had it for forty-eight hours.

The judge excused himself and made his way over to the defendants.

There was no doubt that I was mentally exhausted at this point. After Joy and I talked in private, we decided not to move forward with a trial and ultimately end this chapter of our lives.

When the settlement conference was over, our new lawyer brought us by the Byrne household. When we entered, there were still a lot of family members at the house. We waited in the family room as one of their relatives went to get Margo. My heart was pounding out of my chest, and I was completely sick to my stomach. I wanted to make sure I had the right words to say to her. She had just lost her whole world, and I was sure she was still in shock.

She quickly came, and I introduced her to Joy. She gave us both big hugs and made us feel at ease. I was amazed that she could show such unbelievable grace. She told me how much respect George had for me. He'd taken the case files along with him on vacation because he wanted to make sure he was prepared for the following week. She told me how often they discussed my case and said I'd received a raw deal.

We talked about George and how life had forever changed. The one thing that has stayed with me is when she told us she "had twenty great years with him . . . and that it was just his time." Her perspective in that moment is hard to comprehend, but it was her reality.

I was in shock that, at a time like this, she cared enough to tell me these things. I'm sure she had many other important things on her mind, but it was comforting to know how much he cared about me as a person. It was truly the most humbling experience of my life.

We left the house started our eight-hour journey back home. It seemed like a huge weight was lifted off my shoulders. I couldn't help but think about what Margo said about the twenty great years she'd had with George. Perspective is such an important trait. Life will constantly throw you curveballs. How you respond to adversity is what really matters.

I had a new perspective as this case closed the hockey chapter of my life. I thought back to the journey I'd been on since making that commitment in high school. I'd refused to live with the regret of knowing I didn't do everything possible to achieve my dreams, which most people thought was impossible for me.

For years after my hockey career was over, people would ask me how close I was to making it to the NHL. When I hear that question, I am always reminded of the scene in *Field of Dreams* when Kevin Costner's character asks Moonlight Graham what it was like to be *that close to his dreams*. He had once got called up to the major leagues but never got to bat against a big-league pitcher.

His response: "It's like coming this close to your dreams [indicating inches] and then watch them brush past you like a stranger in the crowd. But at that time, you don't think much of it. You know, we just don't recognize the most significant moments in our lives while they are happening. Back then I thought, well there will be other days. I didn't realize, that was the only day."[2]

Costner would go on to say it would kill most people to get that close to your dream and not touch it. They'd consider it a tragedy.

---

2. Kevin Costner as Moonlight Graham in *Field of Dreams*, directed by Phil Alden Robinson (Lawrence Gordon and Charles Gordon, 1989).

For me, not having done everything in my power to go after my dreams, that would have been the real tragedy.

I can live with the results of my career. Making that life-changing decision the night before the start of my senior year in high school led to many accomplishments that I'm very proud of. Without the decision to commit and not accept being average, my hockey career, no doubt ends in high school. I also wouldn't have the life that I have now. So, did I make it? Getting drafted in the NHL, playing Division I college hockey, playing for my country, signing an NHL contract and going on to play six seasons of professional hockey . . . For me, I did.

I played longer than anyone ever thought I would. I spent twelve great years after high school chasing my goals. I was ready to move on, it was just my time. . . .

Conclusion
Roadmap

"Yesterday is history, tomorrow is a mystery, today is a
gift and that's why we call it the present."
—Unknown

I f you want to succeed at the highest levels in sports, focus
on being a good overall athlete. Play as many sports as you
can, for as long as you can. This will enhance your abilities
but also teach you how to have both successes and failures at
different disciplines. One sport may come naturally to you,
but you might have to work really hard to be good at another.
Learning how to overcome adversity will go a long way in
teaching you to push yourself through obstacles, no matter
where life takes you. And believe me, you are going to face
them.

Set goals and set them high. Challenge yourself to get out
of your comfort zone. When you set a goal, there will be three
possible outcomes:

1) You do everything you can, you reach your goal, and it is awesome.

2) You do everything you can to reach your goal, but for reasons outside of your control, you fall short. While you can do everything possible to control the process, you may not be able to control the outcome. There will always be outside factors at play. This is called disappointment, and it is just part of life. But that is how you live with no regrets.

3) You don't do everything you can, don't push yourself, don't strive to be the best version of yourself, and you live with regret for the rest of your life. In my opinion, that is a terrible thing to live with.

The most important thing to do when setting goals is to commit to them. Then find a way to motivate yourself every day to accomplish them. Everyone is different. I found it in motivational speakers, songs, and movies. Even on the days when I really didn't want to do something, I found a way to motivate myself to push through. Commitment to that ultimate goal will make you find a way.

Take advantage of the moment. Do everything possible to be the best you can be. Be curious about how to get better. Do the research and try different things to improve yourself. If you are doing exactly what everyone else is doing, how will you possibly get better than them? It is one big competition.

As an adult, I often hear people say they should have worked harder in their sports careers when they were younger. I have never heard anyone say they regretted working *too* hard.

I also hear from people on a regular basis that time is flying by. Understand that time goes by faster as you get older. You might not comprehend that now. Just appreciate that one day, you will also feel that way. Make your time count.

Being a great athlete and being successful in a particular sport takes three different skills, which can be represented by a three-legged stool. If any one of the legs is missing or weak, it will eventually tip over and fail. The three legs are:

1) Skills in the specific sport
2) Strength and conditioning
3) Mental mindset and sports-specific IQ

You need to work on all three, or you will not be successful.

It is very important to build what I call a memory bank. Put in it as many positive sports memory deposits as you can. Eventually, when times get tough—and they will—you will need to make a withdrawal. Having a positive memory of how you succeeded in the past will remind you that you can do this. It will push you through adversity and moments when you feel discouraged and want to give up.

There were many times in my career when times got tough and I reached into the bank. Some memories came from different sports, but that didn't matter. They all reminded me that I was capable of great things and that I needed to push through. Nine times out of ten, it worked like a charm. When it didn't, I would keep pushing anyway. The road to success is paved with adversity.

There is a time clock on everyone's sports career. No matter who you are, your career will eventually end. **"Do not quit until you hear the buzzer. At some point, you *will* hear it. But don't press it for your father time."** You have no idea what you are capable of until you push yourself to be the best you can be.

When I look back on my career, I see it differently than I did when I was going through it. Is it tough to reach high levels in sports? The easy answer is yes. But through perspective, I now look back and think it was actually pretty easy. Here is why, and here is your edge:

1) Most people do not truly listen and implement what is being taught to them.
2) Most people give up when it gets really tough.

It is that simple. Listen and put into action what you are learning. Never give up until the buzzer goes off. Most people won't do that. You simply need to outlast them.

Don't settle for being average. It is human nature to be average and seek comfort in being like everyone else. Resist this temptation. There is genius in you. I made a conscious choice to not live with regret, and that led me to not accept being average. Remember, there is no rewind in life.

Many things can happen in an athlete's journey that impact the outcome. It calls for innate talent that you may or may not possess. And injuries are part of the deal when playing competitive sports. Oftentimes, your best ability is your availability.

If you do all of that, you should be content with the results. Ultimately, you do not control the outcome of your career. You can only control your process. Do not *try* your best. Instead, *be* your best.

Eventually, time will run out.

Acknowledgments

To my wife, Joy, and my daughter, Georgia.

To my mom, Jean, and my dad, Bill.

To my siblings: Bill, Deb, Kevin, and Beth.

To all of my teammates and coaches at Cumberland High School, Cushing Academy, UMass Lowell, Saint John Flames, and the Louisiana IceGators.

To the Snodfest crew.

To the UML boys.

To PHC 2009 Hockey Team (2020-2023) and coaches.

To U14/16 RI Sting and coaches.

To Bishop Feehan Girls Hockey and coaches.

To Danielle McDonough.

To David Caissie and Mikey Kershisnik.